contents

The oven temperatures in this book are for conventional ovens; if you have a fan-forced oven, decrease the temperature by 10-20 degrees. A measurement conversion chart appears on the back flap of this book.

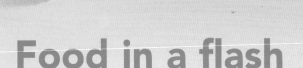

Food in a flash

Everyone's lives are increasingly busy, and people find they have less and less time to cook a healthy and delicious meal. This book was developed because we wanted to show you that it is possible to have a great meal prepared and on the table in 15 minutes. Here are some helpful tips that will keep you feeling calm and in control when you're rushing to get your next meal on the table.

Planning ahead

Being organised is the most important tip that will help you beat the clock when cooking a meal for family and friends. Sit down for half an hour on the weekend and organise what meals you will cook for the week. Write a shopping list for the whole week and try to do the bulk of your grocery shopping on Sunday, allocate any items that need to be purchased on the day and write them in your diary.

Getting organised

Organising your kitchen will make weeknight cooking so much easier. Make sure your most commonly used utensils,

pots and pans are in an easy-to-reach place. Ensure your kitchen equipment is in its best condition and ready to use. Keep your knives sharp to allow for smooth and easy cutting, and don't forget to take advantage of the slicing and grating tools on your food processor. Investing in a 'V' slicer or mandoline will also help speed up the slicing and grating of vegetables – you will be amazed at the time you can save. Finally, don't forget about using your microwave; steam your vegies and add to the side of any dish. There you have it – a nutritious and delicious meal cooked in less than 15 minutes.

Before you start cooking, read the recipe in full, this way you know ahead of time what it is you have to do – making the whole process easier, and faster. Secondly, get out all the pots, pans and other equipment that you will need – do you need to cook pasta? Then fill the kettle and get it boiling ready to pour into the saucepan. If needed, turn on the oven or grill to heat up, or heat oil in the frying pan. Thirdly, prepare all ingredients, including cutting and measuring. Now, you are ready to begin. Remember while you may be pressed for time when you first start, the more you cook these recipes, the faster you will get.

What's at the supermarket?

Today, the supermarket can make your life easier. Don't be afraid to buy prepared foods. In the AWW Test Kitchen our favourite supermarket products are; salad mixes, pre-cut and peeled vegetables, barbecue chickens and stir-fry mixes. These helpful products cut heaps of time from the recipe.

The supermarket is also a great place to buy products that help to achieve your aim of getting a meal on the table in 15 minutes. Pre-made pasta sauces, curry pastes, pizza bases, marinades, salad dressings, coleslaws, salads, pre-mashed potato and sheets of frozen pastry are a few that we find particularly helpful. All you need do with these products is add a few fresh ingredients, and suddenly you have a tasty meal with very little effort.

What's in the pantry?

Sometimes all you need to make a delicious meal is a simple marinade on the meat and a fresh salad. Mix olive oil, garlic and fresh herbs or a blend of the many spices stockpiled in your pantry to give your meal added flavour. For best results, leave meat to marinade overnight. Buy a pre-made salad from the supermarket and there's dinner on the table.

A helping hand…

A lot of butchers today do a brilliant selection of marinated, trimmed, crumbed, skewered and diced meats to help you cut back on preparation times. If you can't find exactly what you are a looking for, simply ask the butcher if he can trim and dice the meat so it is ready for cooking.

Seafood is a great source of healthy omega-3 fatty acids, and has fewer kilojoules than red meat making it a healthy option for your family. The hardest thing about seafood is the cleaning, filleting and shelling. Most fishmongers are happy to do these jobs for you (some fishmongers sell shelled prawns), ensuring that the seafood is quick to cook.

Take advantage of…

Your weekends – soups, pasta sauces, casseroles and curries are good meals to make in big batches on the weekend and then freeze for lunches and easy dinners during the week. Make sure you label and date servings to avoid confusion.

Freeze meals in individual sized portions, making them easy to grab when you're on the go and short of time.

Leftovers – look for meals where the basic ingredients can be made into different meals. For example, bolognaise sauce can become a taco filling with the addition of kidney beans – just add salsa, lettuce, sour cream and cheese. Bolognaise sauce also makes a great cottage pie – top it with pre-mashed potato, sprinkle with cheese and heat in the oven until warmed through and the cheese has melted. In fact, to get it on the table even faster – microwave the bolognaise sauce until hot and place it in a heatproof dish; microwave the potato until hot and it dollop over the sauce, sprinkle with cheese and place the whole thing under a grill, and grill until the cheese is golden brown.

This fantastic collection of delicious 15-minute meals will encourage you to try at least one new speedy recipe each week.

poultry

satay chicken skewers

12 chicken tenderloins (900g)

1 teaspoon curry powder

½ teaspoon each onion and garlic powder

¼ teaspoon each ground cumin and chilli

2 tablespoons peanut oil

1 large brown onion (200g), grated

2 teaspoons crushed ginger

1 cup (250ml) coconut cream

¾ cup (210g) crunchy peanut butter

2 tablespoons sweet chilli sauce

2 tablespoons light soy sauce

¼ cup (35g) crushed roasted peanuts

450g (14½ ounce) packet microwave rice

1 telegraph cucumber (400g), sliced into thin ribbons

1 Heat oiled grill plate (or grill pan or barbecue).

2 Combine chicken, spices and half the oil in large bowl; season. Thread chicken onto 12 bamboo skewers; cook about 3 minutes each side or until cooked.

3 Meanwhile, heat remaining oil in small saucepan. Cook onion and ginger, stirring, about 1 minute or until onion softens. Add coconut cream, peanut butter, sauces and nuts; simmer, stirring, 1 minute.

4 Microwave rice according to packet directions.

5 Top rice with skewers; serve with peanut sauce and cucumber strips. Accompany with some fresh coriander leaves and lime cheeks, if you like.

prep + cook time 15 minutes
serves 4
nutritional count per serving
56.2g total fat
(18.9g saturated fat); 4146kJ
(991 cal); 44.4g carbohydrate;
72.6g protein; 9.7g fibre

notes We used a food processor to grate the onion, a vegetable peeler to slice the cucumber into ribbons, and the crushed ginger available in tubes from supermarkets. Wrap the ends of the bamboo skewers in foil to prevent them burning during cooking.

spiced sesame chicken pieces

peanut oil, for shallow-frying

1½ cups (225g) sesame seeds

800g (1½ pounds) chicken breast fillets

1 teaspoon each ground cumin, coriander, paprika and garlic powder

½ teaspoon ground chilli

2 tablespoons peanut oil, extra

200g (6½ ounces) baby asian greens

1 medium carrot (120g)

sweet soy lime dressing

⅓ cup (80ml) lime juice

⅓ cup (80ml) soy sauce

½ teaspoon sesame oil

1 tablespoon grated palm sugar

1 fresh small red thai chilli (serrano), sliced thinly

1 Heat oil in large frying pan over medium-high heat.
2 Place sesame seeds in a small shallow bowl.
3 Cut each chicken breast fillet into 4 strips. Combine chicken, spices and extra oil in large bowl. Press chicken pieces firmly into sesame seeds to coat.
4 Shallow-fry chicken pieces, in batches, over medium-high heat, until browned lightly and cooked through. Drain on absorbent paper; season.
5 Meanwhile, combine ingredients for sweet soy lime dressing in screw-top jar; shake well.
6 Slice carrot into long thin strips. Combine asian greens and carrot in medium bowl. Serve chicken with salad; accompany with dressing for dipping.

prep + cook time 15 minutes
serves 4
nutritional count per serving
61.1g total fat
(9.3g saturated fat); 3389kJ
(809 cal); 7.4g carbohydrate;
55.1g protein; 5.5g fibre

notes Baby asian greens are a mix of baby buk choy, choy sum, gai lan and water spinach. Use a mandoline or V-slicer with a julienne attachment to slice the carrot into thin strips.

chicken noodle soup

2 green onions (scallions)

1 fresh long red chilli

350g (11 ounces) chicken breast fillets

1 litre (4 cups) chicken consommé

2 tablespoons light soy sauce

200g (6½ ounces) dried egg noodles

½ cup loosely packed fresh coriander (cilantro) leaves

100g (3 ounces) bean sprouts

1 medium lemon, cut into wedges

1 Thinly slice onions and chilli. Thinly slice chicken.
2 Combine consommé, sauce and chilli in medium saucepan; bring to the boil. Reduce heat; simmer. Add chicken; simmer, uncovered, 5 minutes.
3 Meanwhile, cook noodles according to packet directions; divide into 4 serving bowls.
4 Ladle soup into bowls; top with onion, coriander and sprouts; serve with lemon wedges.

prep + cook time 15 minutes
serves 4
nutritional count per serving
3.2g total fat
(1g saturated fat); 1290kJ
(308 cal); 37.9g carbohydrate;
30.1g protein; 2g fibre

note Before starting the recipe, boil the kettle so you have boiling water ready to prepare the noodles.

sweet chilli chicken with mango lime salad

4 chicken breast fillets (800g)

2 tablespoons olive oil

½ cup (125ml) sweet chilli sauce

1 teaspoon bottled crushed garlic

2 tablespoons lime juice

100g (3 ounces) rocket leaves (arugula)

2 limes, halved

mango lime salad

2 medium mangoes (860g), sliced thinly

1 small red onion (100g), sliced thinly

2 tablespoons lime juice

1 long red chilli, chopped finely

1 Heat oiled grill pan (or grill plate or barbecue).

2 Cut chicken breasts in half lengthways.

3 Combine chicken, oil, sauce, garlic and juice in medium bowl; season.

4 Cook chicken, in batches, over medium heat about 2 minutes each side or until cooked.

5 Meanwhile, make mango lime salad. Serve chicken with salad and rocket, and lime cheeks.

MANGO LIME SALAD Combine mango, onion, juice and rocket in medium bowl; gently toss chilli through salad.

prep + cook time 15 minutes
serves 4
nutritional count per serving
13.6g total fat (2.5g saturated fat); 1760kJ (421 cal); 24.1g carbohydrate; 47.4g protein; 4.2g fibre

note You can use a drained and chopped 800g (1½-pound) can of mango cheeks instead of using fresh mango.

Ask the butcher to butterfly the quails for you. Cajun seasoning is available at supermarkets in the spice section. Bottled piquillo peppers are also available at supermarkets, but you can use bottled char-grilled capsicum (bell peppers) if you can't find them. If you don't have a lid that fits your frying pan, use foil instead; make sure the foil doesn't extend over the edge of the pan as it may catch alight.

quails with creamed corn

4 butterflied quails (1.3kg)

¼ cup (60ml) olive oil

2 tablespoons cajun seasoning

1 clove garlic

500g (1 pound) frozen corn kernels

1 cup (240g) sour cream

1 cup (250ml) pouring cream

80g (2½ ounces) drained bottled piquillo peppers

1 lime, cut into cheeks

1 cup loosely packed fresh coriander (cilantro) leaves

1 Rinse quails; pat dry with absorbent paper.

2 Heat 2 tablespoons of the oil in a large frying pan over high heat.

3 Combine quails, remaining oil and seasoning in large bowl; season. Cook quail, skin-side down, 5 minutes or until browned. Reduce heat; turn quail over, cover pan. Cook about 5 minutes or until quail is cooked through.

4 Meanwhile, peel garlic. Combine whole garlic, corn, sour cream and cream in medium saucepan; cook, stirring, until mixture boils. Reduce heat; simmer, uncovered, about 5 minutes or until mixture thickens. Remove from heat; blend with a stick blender until almost smooth. Season to taste.

5 Serve quail with creamed corn mixture; accompany with peppers and lime. Sprinkle over coriander before serving.

prep + cook time 15 minutes
serves 4
nutritional count per serving
74.6g total fat
(37.9g saturated fat); 3734kJ
(892 cal); 33.5g carbohydrate;
21.7g protein; 4.2g fibre

creamy tomato chicken

375g (12 ounces) farfalle (bowtie) pasta

4 chicken breast fillets (800g)

1 tablespoon olive oil

250g (8 ounces) rocket (arugula)

¼ cup each loosely packed fresh basil and oregano leaves

creamy tomato sauce

150g (5 ounces) button mushrooms

1 tablespoon olive oil

1 teaspoon bottled crushed garlic

400g (12½ ounces) canned crushed tomatoes

½ cup (125ml) pouring cream

1 Cook pasta in large saucepan of boiling water until tender; drain.
2 Meanwhile, make creamy tomato sauce.
3 Cut chicken breasts in half horizontally. Heat oil in large frying pan; cook chicken, in batches, over high heat, about 3 minutes each side or until cooked.
4 Serve chicken with pasta and rocket; drizzle with sauce, sprinkle over fresh herbs.

CREAMY TOMATO SAUCE Thinly slice mushrooms. Heat oil in medium saucepan; cook mushrooms and garlic, stirring, until mushrooms are tender. Add undrained tomatoes. Simmer, uncovered, 5 minutes. Add cream; simmer, uncovered, 1 minute. Season to taste.

prep + cook time 15 minutes **serves** 4
nutritional count per serving 24.6g total fat (9.6g saturated fat); 2372kJ (567 cal); 30.1g carbohydrate; 52.9g protein; 5.2g fibre

note Before starting the recipe, boil the kettle so you have boiling water ready to go into the saucepan to cook the pasta.

asparagus and smoked chicken salad

175g (5½ ounces) asparagus, trimmed

350g (11 ounces) watercress

1 large avocado (320g)

200g (6½ ounces) yellow grape tomatoes

450g (14½ ounces) smoked chicken breast

⅔ cup (160g) sour cream

⅔ cup (160ml) buttermilk

2 tablespoons finely grated lemon rind

⅓ cup loosely packed fresh tarragon leaves

1 Halve asparagus lengthways. Boil, steam or microwave asparagus until tender; drain.
2 Meanwhile, trim watercress. Thinly slice avocado. Halve tomatoes. Thinly slice chicken.
3 To make dressing, combine sour cream, buttermilk and rind in small jug; season to taste.
4 Combine asparagus, watercress, avocado, tomato and chicken on serving plates. Drizzle with dressing; sprinkle with tarragon.

prep + cook time 15 minutes **serves** 4
nutritional count per serving 33.5g total fat (15.1g saturated fat); 1940kJ (464 cal); 5.7g carbohydrate; 33.4g protein; 3.5g fibre

honey horseradish glazed chicken

½ cup (140g) horseradish cream

2 tablespoons honey

2 teaspoons bottled crushed garlic

2 tablespoons white wine vinegar

2 tablespoons olive oil

2 tablespoons water

8 chicken thigh fillets (1kg)

400g (12½ ounce) packet asian salad mix

1 Heat oiled grill plate (or grill pan or barbecue).
2 Combine horseradish, honey, garlic, vinegar, oil and water in small bowl; season.
3 Pound thickest part of chicken with a mallet. Brush chicken with glaze; cook, turning and basting with glaze, about 10 minutes or until cooked.
4 Serve chicken with salad, and any reserved glaze.

prep + cook time 15 minutes
serves 4
nutritional count per serving
36.7g total fat
(9g saturated fat); 2699kJ
(645 cal); 30.4g carbohydrate;
49g protein; 0.8g fibre

serving suggestion The chicken would also go well with a potato or green leafy salad.

chicken sausages with sage and onion gravy

2 tablespoons olive oil

8 chicken sausages (1kg)

2 x 475g (15-ounce) tubs mashed potato with cheese

200g rocket leaves (arugula)

sage and onion gravy

2 tablespoons olive oil

1 teaspoon bottled crushed garlic

½ cup (150g) caramelised onion

1 tablespoon plain (all-purpose) flour

1 cup (250ml) chicken stock

8 fresh sage leaves

⅓ cup (80ml) apple cider

1 Heat oil in large frying pan; cook sausages over medium heat, turning, about 10 minutes or until cooked through.

2 Meanwhile, make sage and onion gravy.

3 Microwave mashed potato according to directions on tub.

4 Drizzle sausages with sage and onion gravy; serve with rocket and mashed potato. Sprinkle with extra sage leaves, if you like.

SAGE AND ONION GRAVY

Heat oil in medium saucepan; cook garlic and caramelised onion until fragrant. Add flour; cook, stirring, 1 minute. Gradually add stock, then torn sage leaves and cider; simmer, uncovered, about 10 minutes or until gravy is thickened slightly. Season to taste.

prep + cook time 15 minutes
serves 4
nutritional count per serving
81.4g total fat
(24.6 saturated fat); 4544kJ
(1085 cal); 42.8g carbohydrate;
40.8g protein; 11.3g fibre

notes Larger supermarkets stock ready-mashed potato; you will find it either in the freezer or refrigerated sections. Jars of caramelised onion can be found in the condiment aisle.

thyme chicken with mustard cheese sauce

10 sprigs fresh thyme

1kg (2 pounds) chicken tenderloins

2 teaspoons bottled crushed garlic

2 tablespoons olive oil

25g (¾ ounce) butter

2 tablespoons plain (all-purpose) flour

1¾ cups (410ml) milk

3 teaspoons dijon mustard

¾ cup (90g) coarsely grated cheddar cheese

1 bunch baby carrots (400g)

500g (1 pound) packet frozen peas

100g (3 ounces) butter extra, softened

1 Preheat grill (broiler). Remove thyme leaves from sprigs; combine thyme leaves, chicken, garlic and oil in large bowl, season.
2 Place chicken on large oven tray; grill about 10 minutes or until cooked, turning halfway through cooking.
3 Meanwhile, to make mustard cheese sauce: melt butter in medium saucepan. Add flour; cook, stirring, about 30 seconds. Gradually add milk; cook, stirring, about 3 minutes or until sauce boils and thickens. Remove from heat; stir in mustard and cheese. Season to taste.
4 Trim and peel carrots. Microwave carrots and peas separately until tender. Mash peas with extra butter.
5 Serve chicken with vegetables; accompany with mustard cheese sauce.

prep + cook time 15 minutes **serves** 4
nutritional count per serving 51.1g total fat (27g saturated fat); 3610kJ (862 cal); 21.5g carbohydrate; 74.1g protein; 13.3g fibre

note You could also serve this recipe with a mixed leaf salad.

margarita chicken

1 lime

8 chicken thigh fillets (1kg)

1 teaspoon dried chilli flakes

2 teaspoons bottled crushed garlic

2 tablespoons olive oil

500g (1 pound) cherry truss tomatoes

2 tablespoons tequila

2 tablespoons olive oil, extra

1 tablespoon caster (superfine) sugar

2 cups loosely packed fresh coriander leaves (cilantro)

450g (14½-ounce) packet microwave rice

1 Heat oiled grill plate (or grill pan or barbecue). Preheat grill (broiler).
2 Cut lime rind into thin strips; squeeze juice from lime. Combine rind, chicken, chilli, garlic and oil in large bowl; season.
3 Cook chicken on grill plate about 5 minutes each side or until cooked through.
4 Meanwhile, grill tomatoes until just beginning to split.
5 Combine juice, tequila, extra oil, sugar and coriander in large bowl; season to taste.
6 Microwave rice according to packet directions.
7 Serve chicken with rice; top with tomatoes and tequila mixture. Accompany with lime wedges, if you like.

prep + cook time 15 minutes **serves** 4
nutritional count per serving 36.7g total fat (8.1g saturated fat); 2742kJ (655 cal); 25.7g carbohydrate; 48.7g protein; 2.9g fibre

note A green leafy salad would also go well with this recipe.

malaysian chicken curry

2 medium potatoes (400g)
(see note)

1 tablespoon vegetable oil

1 medium brown onion (150g)

2 teaspoons bottled crushed
garlic

500g (1 pound) chicken breast
stir-fry strips

1 cinnamon stick

2 x 410g (13 ounces) canned
mild malaysian curry sauce

200g (6½ ounces) baby green
beans

⅓ cup (45g) roasted peanuts

750g (1½ pounds) microwavable
long-grain white rice

½ cup coarsely chopped fresh
coriander (cilantro)

1 Place unpeeled potatoes in microwave-safe bowl; microwave on HIGH (100%) for 5 minutes. Cut potatoes into wedges.
2 Meanwhile, heat oil in large deep frying pan over high heat. Thinly slice onion. Cook onion and garlic, stirring, until onion softens.
3 Add chicken, cinnamon, sauce and potatoes to pan; bring to the boil. Reduce heat; simmer, uncovered, about 5 minutes or until chicken is cooked.
4 Meanwhile, microwave beans until just tender.
5 Coarsely chop nuts. Microwave rice according to directions on packet. Remove cinnamon stick from curry. Serve curry topped with beans, nuts and coriander; accompany with rice.

prep + cook time 15 minutes
serves 6
nutritional count per serving
23.4g total fat
(10.1g saturated fat); 2046kJ
(489 cal); 55g carbohydrate;
9.5g protein; 6.5g fibre

note We used desiree potatoes for this recipe and left the skins on; use any potato you like. Baby new potatoes (chats), would also work well in this recipe.

chicken parmigiana stacks

4 slices prosciutto (60g)

2 tablespoons olive oil

4 chicken minute steaks (320g)

4 bocconcini cheese (100g)

400g (12½ ounces) canned cherry tomatoes

4 slices char-grilled eggplant (100g)

¼ cup loosely packed fresh cress or baby basil leaves

1 Preheat grill (broiler). Place prosciutto on baking-paper-lined oven tray; place under grill. Grill about 3 minutes or until prosciutto is browned and crisp. Remove from grill; cover to keep warm. Leave grill on.
2 Meanwhile, heat half the oil in shallow 2-litre (8-cup) flameproof baking dish over medium-high heat on stove top. Season chicken; cook about 1 minute each side or until almost cooked through, remove from heat. Remove chicken from dish.
3 Slice cheese thinly. Add undrained tomatoes to dish; place chicken on top. Top chicken with eggplant and cheese.
4 Place baking dish under grill; cook about 3 minutes or until cheese melts and chicken is cooked through.
5 To serve, spoon tomato over the chicken stacks, top with prosciutto and cress; drizzle with remaining oil.

prep + cook time 15 minutes
serves 4
nutritional count per serving
15.4g total fat
(4.5g saturated fat); 1104kJ
(264 cal); 4.3g carbohydrate;
26.1g protein; 2.3g fibre

notes Put the baking dish as close to the preheated grill as possible. This dish can be served as is, or accompany it with a salad, or soft polenta, and fresh crusty bread to soak up the juices.

turkey with pistachio and cabbage salad

⅓ cup (45g) unsalted shelled pistachios

1 tablespoon olive oil

4 turkey breast steaks (440g)

20g (¾ ounce) butter

¼ medium red cabbage (375g)

2 witlof (250g), quartered lengthways

¼ cup loosely packed fresh flat-leaf parsley leaves

⅓ cup (45g) dried cranberries

⅓ cup (80ml) honey mustard dressing

1 Dry-fry nuts in large frying pan, stirring, over high heat until browned lightly and fragrant; transfer to small bowl.

2 Add oil to pan; season turkey, cook about 4 minutes each side, over high heat, or until cooked through. Add butter to pan; turn to coat turkey in butter.

3 Meanwhile, to make salad, finely shred cabbage. Coarsely chop nuts. Combine cabbage, witlof, nuts, parsley and cranberries in large bowl; season to taste.

4 Serve turkey with salad; drizzle with dressing. Sprinkle with extra parsley, if you like.

prep + cook time 10 minutes
serves 4
nutritional count per serving
23.1g total fat
(5.5g saturated fat); 1670kJ
(399 cal); 15.6g carbohydrate;
29.3g protein; 7g fibre

chicken fajitas

500g (1 pound) chicken breast
stir-fry strips

½ teaspoon each ground
cumin, coriander, chilli and
smoked paprika

2 tablespoons olive oil

1 large red capsicum
(bell pepper) (350g)

1 large yellow capsicum
(bell pepper) (350g)

1 medium red onion (170g)

½ cup loosely packed fresh
coriander (cilantro) leaves

¼ cup (60ml) water

12 x 19cm (7¾-inch) flour
tortillas

1 cup (240g) sour cream

1 lime

1 Combine chicken, spices and
half the oil in large bowl; season.
2 Thinly slice capsicums and
onion. Finely chop half the
coriander.
3 Heat remaining oil in large
frying pan; cook capsicum and
onion, stirring, over high heat,
about 5 minutes or until soft.
Add the chopped coriander;
transfer to a medium bowl, cover
to keep warm.
4 Add chicken to pan; cook,
stirring, until browned and cooked
through. Return capsicum mixture
to pan with the water; cook,
stirring, until hot. Season to taste.
5 Meanwhile, heat tortillas in
microwave according to directions
on packet.
6 Serve chicken with tortillas,
sour cream, lime wedges and
remaining coriander.

prep + cook time 15 minutes
serves 4
nutritional count per serving
42.4g total fat
(18.9g saturated fat); 3370kJ
(805 cal); 62.6g carbohydrate;
41g protein; 5.4g fibre

notes Increase the amount of
chilli powder, if you want a little
extra heat.
You could also heat the tortillas
on a grill plate, if you like; spray
the tortillas with a little oil.

lamb

lamb with middle-eastern-style couscous

1 cup (200g) couscous

1 cup (250ml) boiling water

20g (¾ ounce) butter

700g (1½ pounds) lamb backstrap

1 tablespoon olive oil

1 medium carrot (120g)

½ cup (125ml) pomegranate pulp

1 teaspoon ground cumin

½ teaspoon sumac

1 cup loosely packed fresh mint

200g (6½ ounces) tzatziki

1 teaspoon extra virgin olive oil

pinch sumac, extra

1 medium lemon (140g)

1 Heat oiled grill pan (or grill plate or barbecue).

2 Meanwhile, combine couscous, the water and butter in medium heatproof bowl, cover; stand about 5 minutes or until liquid is absorbed, fluffing with fork occasionally.

3 Rub lamb with oil, season; cook about 4 minutes each side or until cooked as desired. Remove from pan, cover; stand 5 minutes, then slice thinly.

4 Meanwhile, slice carrot into thin strips about 5cm (2-inches) long. Stir carrot, pulp, spices and mint into couscous. Season to taste.

5 Drizzle oil over tzatziki, sprinkle over extra sumac. Serve lamb with couscous; accompany with tzatziki and lemon wedges.

prep + cook time 15 minutes
serves 4
nutritional count per serving
24.6g total fat
(8.8g saturated fat); 2769kJ
(661 cal); 45.6g carbohydrate;
61.3g protein; 5.5g fibre

notes To remove the seeds/pulp from pomegranate, cut it in half crossways and hold each half cut-side down over a bowl. Hit the outside skin of the fruit sharply with a wooden spoon – as hard as you can – the seeds should fall out – if they don't, dig them out with a teaspoon. Be careful seeding pomegranate as the juice can stain your hands and bench top. Use a mandoline or V-slicer with a julienne attachment to cut the carrots into matchsticks.

quince, rosemary and red wine glazed lamb

2 sprigs fresh rosemary

2 lamb backstraps (400g)

1 tablespoon olive oil

100g (3 ounces) quince paste

1 teaspoon bottled crushed garlic

1 cup (250ml) dry red wine

200g (6½ ounces) green beans

2 x 475g (15-ounce) tubs mashed potato

1 Heat large frying pan over medium-high heat.

2 Remove leaves from rosemary sprigs; chop finely. Combine rosemary, lamb and oil in medium bowl; season.

3 Cook lamb about 3 minutes each side or until cooked as desired. Remove from pan, cover; stand 5 minutes.

4 Add quince paste to same heated pan; cook, stirring, over medium heat, until softened. Add garlic and wine to pan; cook, stirring, until mixture is combined. Simmer, uncovered, about 3 minutes or until the glaze has thickened.

5 Meanwhile, microwave beans until just tender; drain.

6 Microwave mashed potato according to directions on tub.

7 Slice lamb thinly; serve drizzled with glaze. Accompany with beans and potato, top with freshly ground black pepper.

prep + cook time 15 minutes
serves 4
nutritional count per serving 22.3g total fat (10.5g saturated fat); 2148kJ (513 cal); 38.4g carbohydrate; 36g protein; 5.6g fibre

serving suggestion You could add steamed baby carrots.

lamb with crumbed eggplant and pesto

¼ cup (60g) olive oil

12 french-trimmed lamb cutlets (600g)

1 egg

2 tablespoons milk

2 tablespoons plain (all-purpose) flour

1½ cups (100g) panko (japanese) breadcrumbs

1 medium eggplant (300g)

⅓ cup pesto (90g)

1 tablespoon olive oil, extra

250g (8 ounces) rocket leaves (arugula)

1 Heat oil in large frying pan over high heat. Season lamb; cook in pan until cooked as desired. Remove from pan; cover to keep warm.

2 Meanwhile, lightly beat egg in shallow bowl. Place flour and breadcrumbs in separate shallow bowls.

3 Thickly slice eggplant; pat dry with absorbent paper. Dip eggplant in flour, shake off excess, then dip in egg, then breadcrumbs to coat. Cook eggplant, in batches, until browned lightly both sides. Drain on absorbent paper.

4 Drizzle pesto with extra oil. Serve lamb with eggplant and rocket; accompany with pesto.

prep + cook time 15 minutes
serves 4
nutritional count per serving
46.2g total fat
(12.3g saturated fat); 2609kJ
(623 cal); 26.6g carbohydrate;
24.5g protein; 3.4g fibre

note Store-bought pesto is available from the refrigerated section of most supermarkets (near the dips). You will also find it in the pasta aisle.

lebanese-style lamb cutlets

2 tablespoons olive oil

8 french-trimmed lamb cutlets (400g)

¼ cup (60ml) lemon juice

½ teaspoon cracked black pepper

½ teaspoon ground cinnamon

¼ teaspoon each paprika and ground cumin

2 teaspoons bottled crushed garlic

1 large orange (300g)

½ cup (130g) hummus

¼ cup loosely packed fresh mint leaves

1 Heat oil in large frying pan over high heat.
2 Combine lamb, juice, pepper, spices and garlic in large bowl. Cook lamb about 3 minutes each side or until cooked as desired.
3 Thickly slice orange.
4 Sprinkle hummus with a little extra paprika and cumin. Sprinkle mint over orange slices; serve lamb with orange and hummus.

prep + cook time 15 minutes
serves 4
nutritional count per serving
24.7g total fat
(5.6g saturated fat); 1468kJ
(351 cal); 10.9g carbohydrate;
17.5g protein; 7.6g fibre

notes Hummus is a Middle-Eastern dip made from chickpeas, garlic, lemon juice and tahini (sesame seed paste); it can be purchased, ready-made, from most delicatessens and supermarkets.
Cut the orange into wedges and toss them through a green salad mix, if you like.

barbecued moroccan lamb patties

2 tablespoons olive oil

½ medium red capsicum
(bell pepper) (100g)

1 small brown onion (80g)

500g (1 pound) minced (ground)
lamb

1 egg

½ cup (50g) packaged
breadcrumbs

1 teaspoon bottled crushed
garlic

1 tablespoon moroccan spice mix

½ cup loosely packed fresh
coriander leaves (cilantro)

1 cup (200g) couscous

1 cup (250ml) boiling water

20g (¾ ounce) butter

125g (4 ounces) canned
chickpeas (garbanzo beans)

200g (6½ ounce) tub tzatziki

1 Heat oil on large barbecue
flat plate.
2 Finely chop capsicum and
onion. Combine lamb, onion,
capsicum, egg, breadcrumbs,
garlic, spice and half the coriander
in medium bowl; season. Shape
mixture into 8 patties; cook patties
about 5 minutes each side or until
browned and cooked. Drain on
absorbent paper.
3 Meanwhile, combine couscous,
the water and butter in medium
heatproof bowl, cover; stand
about 5 minutes or until liquid
is absorbed, fluffing with fork
occasionally.
4 Rinse and drain chickpeas;
stir chickpeas and remaining
coriander through couscous.
Serve patties with couscous;
accompany with tzatziki.

prep + cook time 15 minutes
serves 4
nutritional count per serving
30.6g total fat
(10.9g saturated fat); 2312kJ
(552 cal); 30.6g carbohydrate;
37.8g protein; 4.4g fibre

notes You can also cook the
patties, in batches, in a large
frying pan. Accompany with
tortillas, if you like.

lamb steaks with mushroom cream sauce

4 lamb steaks (600g)

2 tablespoons olive oil

mushroom cream sauce

100g (3 ounces) button mushrooms

30g (1 ounce) butter

2 teaspoons bottled crushed garlic

¼ cup (60ml) dry white wine

1 tablespoon balsamic vinegar

1¼ cups (310ml) thickened (heavy) cream (see notes)

350g (11 ounces) broccolini

1 Heat oiled grill pan (or grill plate or barbecue).

2 Rub lamb with oil, season. Cook lamb about 2 minutes each side or until cooked as desired. Remove from heat, cover; stand 5 minutes.

3 Meanwhile, make mushroom cream sauce.

4 Microwave broccolini until just tender.

5 Serve lamb with broccolini; drizzle with sauce.

MUSHROOM CREAM SAUCE

Thinly slice mushrooms. Melt butter in medium frying pan; cook mushrooms and garlic, stirring, until tender. Add wine and vinegar; simmer, uncovered, until liquid is reduced by half. Add cream; simmer, uncovered, until sauce thickens. Season to taste.

prep + cook time 15 minutes
serves 4
nutritional count per serving
53.1g total fat
(27.3g saturated fat); 2765kJ
(661 cal); 3.4g carbohydrate;
39.1g protein; 4g fibre

notes It is fine to use just one 300ml tub of cream for this recipe. We used 2 bunches of broccolini. Accompany with mashed potato, if you like. Larger supermarkets stock ready-made mashed potato; you will find it in the freezer or refrigerated sections of the supermarket.

mustard and parmesan-crusted lamb cutlets

12 x frenched lamb cutlets
(600g)

1 tablespoon dijon mustard

½ cup (40g) finely grated
parmesan cheese

400g (12½ ounces) baby new
potatoes

340g (11 ounces) asparagus,
trimmed

2 tablespoons olive oil

1 tablespoon finely chopped
flat-leaf parsley

1 medium lemon (140g)

1 Preheat grill (broiler).
2 Place lamb on oiled oven tray;
season. Grill 3 minutes. Turn
lamb; spread uncooked side with
mustard, sprinkle with cheese.
Grill about 2 minutes or until
browned lightly and cooked.
3 Boil, steam or microwave
potato and asparagus, separately,
until tender. When potato has
cooled slightly, slice thickly. Toss
potato, oil and parsley in large
bowl to combine; season to taste.
4 Serve lamb with asparagus
and potato; accompany with
lemon wedges.

prep + cook time 15 minutes
serves 4
nutritional count per serving
38.9g total fat
(15.6g saturated fat); 2072kJ
(495 cal); 14.6g carbohydrate;
20.6g protein; 3.1g fibre

lamb burgers with caper and herb mayonnaise

1 tablespoon olive oil

250g (8 ounces) minced (ground) lamb

¼ cup loosely packed fresh flat-leaf parsley leaves

2 tablespoons fresh dill sprigs

2 teaspoons rinsed, drained capers

½ small red onion (50g)

½ cup (150g) mayonnaise

1 teaspoon lemon juice

1 large tomato (220g)

2 white bread rolls (180g)

30g (1 ounces) baby spinach leaves

1 Heat oil in medium frying pan over medium heat.

2 Season lamb in medium bowl; shape mixture into 2 patties. Cook patties about 4 minutes each side or until cooked through.

3 Meanwhile, to make caper and herb mayonnaise: Coarsely chop herbs and capers together. Finely chop onion. Combine herb mixture, onion, mayonnaise and juice in small bowl.

4 Slice tomato thinly. Split buns; spread with caper and herb mayonnaise. Sandwich patties, tomato and spinach between buns.

prep + cook time 15 minutes
makes 2
nutritional count per burger
45.2g total fat
(8.8g saturated fat); 3336kJ
(798 cal); 59.7g carbohydrate;
35.9g protein; 6g fibre

rosemary lamb skewers with white bean purée

2 tablespoons olive oil

8 long sprigs fresh rosemary

800g (1½ pounds) diced lamb

40g (1½ ounces) butter

800g (1½ pounds) canned white beans, rinsed, drained

1 teaspoon bottled crushed garlic

2 tablespoons lemon juice

200g (6½ ounces) baby green beans

1 Heat oil in large frying pan over medium-high heat.

2 Remove rosemary leaves from sprigs, leaving 4cm (1½ inches) at the top. Finely chop 2 tablespoons of the rosemary leaves. Thread lamb pieces onto rosemary skewers; season.

3 Cook skewers about 8 minutes, turning, until browned all over and cooked as desired. Remove from pan, cover; stand 5 minutes.

4 Melt half the butter in medium saucepan. Add white beans to pan with garlic; cook, stirring, about 3 minutes or until hot. Stir in juice. Blend or process bean mixture until smooth (add a little boiling water if mixture is too thick). Season to taste.

5 Meanwhile, microwave green beans until tender. Cover to keep warm.

6 Add remaining butter and the chopped rosemary to same frying pan; cook, stirring, about 1 minute or until butter is browned lightly and smells nutty, taking care not to burn the rosemary.

7 Serve lamb skewers with white bean purée and beans; drizzle with rosemary brown butter.

prep + cook time 15 minutes
serves 4
nutritional count per serving
31.8g total fat
(13.5g saturated fat); 2404kJ
(574 cal); 17.8g carbohydrate;
51.2g protein; 10.1g fibre

note We used cannellini beans but you can use any canned white beans you like.

grilled lamb chops with celeriac remoulade

4 lamb forequarter chops (1kg)

¼ cup (90g) honey

2 tablespoons olive oil

2 teaspoons bottled crushed garlic

1 tablespoon fresh thyme leaves

2 teaspoons cracked black pepper

1 celeriac (celery root) (750g)

½ cup (150g) mayonnaise

2 tablespoons finely chopped fresh chervil

1 tablespoon each finely chopped fresh tarragon and chives

2 tablespoons lemon juice

1 Heat oiled grill plate (or grill pan or barbecue).
2 Combine lamb, honey, oil, garlic, thyme and pepper in large bowl; season. Cook lamb about 5 minutes each side or until cooked as desired.
3 Meanwhile, trim and peel celeriac; cut celeriac into matchsticks. Combine celeriac and remaining ingredients in medium bowl; season to taste.
4 Serve lamb with remoulade.

prep + cook time 15 minutes
serves 4
nutritional count per serving
32.2g total fat
(7.8g saturated fat); 2504kJ
(599 cal); 33.6g carbohydrate;
40.5g protein; 8.4g fibre

notes Use a mandoline or V-slicer with a julienne attachment to cut the celeriac into thin strips. Add some mixed salad greens, if you like.

lamb with beetroot pilaf

600g (1¼ pounds) lamb
backstraps

1 tablespoon lemon juice

1 tablespoon olive oil

1 teaspoon fresh thyme leaves

450g (14½-ounce) packet
microwave white long-grain rice

1 cup (200g) beetroot dip

120g (4 ounces) soft goat's
cheese

1 cup loosely packed fresh mint

50g beetroot leaves

1 medium lemon (140g)

1 Heat grill plate (or grill pan
or barbecue).
2 Combine lamb, juice, oil and
thyme in medium bowl; season.
Cook lamb, over medium heat,
about 5 minutes each side or until
cooked as desired. Remove from
heat, cover; stand 5 minutes.
3 Meanwhile, heat rice according
to directions on packet. Heat dip
in microwave until heated through.
Stir dip through hot rice; season
to taste.
4 Slice lamb thinly; serve with
pilaf, sprinkle over cheese, mint,
and leaves. Accompany with
lemon wedges.

prep + cook time 15 minutes
serves 4
nutritional count per serving
18.7g total fat
(7.4g saturated fat); 2212kJ
(528 cal); 35.9g carbohydrate;
51.5g protein; 2.8g fibre

lamb biryani

1 medium brown onion (150g)

500g (1 pound) lamb stir-fry strips

¼ cup (60g) ghee (see note)

1 cinnamon stick

4 cardamom pods

1½ teaspoons garam masala

½ teaspoon ground turmeric

2 tablespoons blanched almonds

450g (14½-ounce) packet microwave basmati rice

¼ teaspoon saffron threads

⅓ cup (50g) raisins

⅓ cup loosely packed fresh coriander leaves (cilantro)

1 packet pappadams (100g)

mint raita

½ cup finely chopped fresh mint

200g (6½ ounces) plain yogurt

pinch ground cumin

1 Make raita.
2 Thinly slice onion. Coarsely chop lamb strips.
3 Preheat grill (broiler).
4 Heat ghee in large saucepan; cook onion, cinnamon, cardamom, garam masala and turmeric, stirring, over medium-high heat about 2 minutes or until onion is softened and browned lightly. Add lamb; cook, stirring, about 2 minutes or until browned.
5 Meanwhile, place almonds on oven tray; roast under grill until just golden. Remove from heat; cool, then chop coarsely.
6 Heat rice according to directions on packet.
7 Remove pan from heat. Stir rice, saffron and raisins into lamb mixture. Season to taste. Discard cinnamon stick before serving.
8 Microwave pappadams according to packet directions. Sprinkle biryani with coriander and nuts; serve immediately, accompanied by mint raita and pappadams.

MINT RAITA Combine ingredients in small bowl.

prep + cook time 15 minutes
serves 4
nutritional count per serving
28.1g total fat (15.6g saturated fat); 2688kJ (642 cal); 56.1g carbohydrate; 38.3g protein; 2.6g fibre

note Use olive oil instead of ghee, if you like.

beef & veal

thai beef salad

500g (1 pound) beef sirloin steak

1 fresh small red thai (serrano) chilli

1 lime

2 tablespoons fish sauce

1 tablespoon grated palm sugar

2 tablespoons sesame oil

1 telegraph (hothouse) cucumber (400g)

2 medium tomatoes (300g)

1 medium red onion (170g)

1 medium grapefruit (425g)

1 cup loosely packed fresh mint leaves

1 cup loosely packed fresh basil leaves

¼ cup (10g) flaked coconut

1 Heat oiled medium frying pan over medium-high heat. Cook beef about 4 minutes each side or until cooked as desired. Remove from heat, cover; stand 5 minutes.

2 Meanwhile, finely slice chilli lengthways. Finely grate lime (you need 1 teaspoon rind); squeeze juice (you need 2 tablespoons juice). Whisk chilli, rind, juice, sauce, sugar and oil in small bowl until combined. Transfer half the dressing to medium bowl.

3 Slice beef thinly, add to dressing in medium bowl; toss to combine.

4 Thinly slice cucumber, tomato and onion. Segment grapefruit. Combine tomato, cucumber, onion, grapefruit, herbs, beef and remaining dressing in large bowl; season to taste. Serve sprinkled with coconut.

prep + cook time 15 minutes
serves 4
nutritional count per serving
15.3g total fat
(4.1g saturated fat); 1436kJ
(343 cal); 13.5g carbohydrate;
34.7g protein; 5.3g fibre

scotch fillet steak with anchovy butter

1 medium lemon (140g

100g (3 ounces) cold butter

1 teaspoon smoked paprika

3 drained anchovy fillets

1 tablespoon finely chopped fresh flat-leaf parsley

4 beef scotch fillet steaks (800g)

2 tablespoons olive oil

350g (11 ounces) watercress

⅔ cup (180g) drained char-grilled capsicum strips

1 Finely grate lemon rind (you need 1 teaspoon); squeeze juice (you need 2 tablespoons).

2 Coarsely chop butter. Process butter, paprika, anchovies, parsley, rind and half the juice until combined. Transfer butter mixture to a piece of plastic wrap; shape into log, roll tightly. Freeze until ready to use.

3 Heat oiled grill plate (or grill pan or barbecue). Rub beef with half the oil; season. Cook beef about 4 minutes each side or until cooked as desired. Remove from heat, cover; stand 5 minutes.

4 Trim watercress; combine with capsicum, remaining oil and juice in large bowl. Season to taste.

5 Serve beef topped with a slice of anchovy butter; accompany with watercress salad.

prep + cook time 15 minutes
serves 4
nutritional count per serving
44.4g total fat
(19.7g saturated fat); 2533kJ
(606 cal); 2.7g carbohydrate;
48.7g protein; 1.2g fibre

sichuan steak with mushroom salad

1 tablespoon sichuan peppercorns

1 tablespoon sea salt

4 thin beef scotch fillet steaks (800g)

¼ cup (60ml) olive oil

1 medium fennel bulb (300g)

250g (8 ounces) button mushrooms

1 fresh small red thai (serrano) chilli

2 green onions (scallions)

1 medium lemon (140g)

450g (14½-ounce) packet microwave rice

2 tablespoons light soy sauce

80g (2½ ounces) baby spinach leaves

⅓ cup loosely packed fresh mint leaves

1 Heat oiled grill plate (or grill pan or barbecue).

2 Grind pepper and salt in mortar and pestle until coarse. Combine beef, 1 tablespoon of the oil, and the pepper mixture in medium bowl. Cook beef about 5 minutes each side or until cooked. Remove from heat, cover; stand 5 minutes.

3 Meanwhile, trim fennel. Thinly slice fennel, mushrooms and chilli. Coarsely chop onions. Finely grate lemon rind (you need 1 teaspoon rind); squeeze juice (you need 1 tablespoon juice).

4 Heat rice according to directions on packet.

5 Whisk rind, juice, sauce and remaining oil in large bowl until combined. Add fennel, mushrooms, onion, chilli and spinach; toss gently. Season to taste.

6 Slice beef thinly; serve with salad, sprinkle with mint.

prep + cook time 15 minutes
serves 4
nutritional count per serving
25.9g total fat
(6.6g saturated fat); 2470kJ
(590 cal); 33.4g carbohydrate;
52.8g protein; 4.6g fibre

steak sandwich with caramelised onion

2 tablespoons olive oil

2 teaspoons cracked black pepper

4 beef minute steaks (400g)

1 loaf turkish bread (430g)

⅓ cup (100g) aïoli

½ cup (70g) caramelised onion relish

½ cup loosely packed trimmed watercress

1 Heat oiled grill pan (or grill or barbecue).

2 Combine oil and pepper in shallow dish; add beef, turn to coat. Cook beef about 2 minutes each side or until cooked as desired. Remove from heat, cover; stand 5 minutes.

3 Meanwhile, cut bread crossways into 4 pieces; split in half and toast cut sides. Spread aïoli onto toasted sides of bread; top four slices with beef, onion relish and watercress then top with remaining bread.

prep + cook time 15 minutes
makes 4
nutritional count per sandwich
37.1g total fat
(7g saturated fat); 2805kJ
(671 cal); 51.6g carbohydrate;
31.5g protein; 3.4g fibre

note Aïoli is a garlic mayonnaise available from the condiment aisle in most supermarkets.

teriyaki and mustard-glazed chipolatas

2 teaspoons olive oil

16 beef chipolata sausages (480g)

½ cup (125ml) thick teriyaki sauce

½ cup (125ml) water

1 tablespoon hot english mustard

250g (8-ounce) packet rice stick noodles

2 green onions (shallots)

½ cup loosely packed fresh coriander (cilantro) leaves

1 Heat oil over medium heat in large frying pan; cook sausages, turning, about 5 minutes or until browned all over.
2 Add sauce, the water and mustard; cook, stirring occasionally, about 2 minutes or until sausages are cooked and the sauce thickens.
3 Place noodles in large heatproof bowl, cover with boiling water; stand until tender, drain.
4 Meanwhile, thinly slice onions.
5 Slice sausages lengthways on the diagonal; serve with noodles, sprinkle over coriander and onion.

prep + cook time 15 minutes
serves 4
nutritional count per serving
33.1g total fat
(15g saturated fat); 1820kJ
(435 cal); 15.8g carbohydrate;
17g protein; 3.8g fibre

note Before starting the recipe, boil the kettle so you have boiling water ready to prepare the noodles.

spicy steak fajitas

400g (12½ ounces) beef stir-fry strips

¼ cup (60ml) olive oil

1 tablespoon ground cumin

3 teaspoons sweet paprika

1 tablespoon dried oregano

2 tablespoons lime juice

1 medium red onion (170g)

1 medium red capsicum (bell pepper) (200g)

1 teaspoon bottled crushed garlic

4 x 20cm (8-inch) flour tortillas

⅓ cup (80g) sour cream

1 medium avocado (250g)

250g (8 ounces) cherry tomatoes

½ cup (60g) grated cheddar cheese

1 lime

1 Heat oiled large frying pan over high heat.

2 Combine beef, oil, spices, oregano and juice in large bowl; season. Cook beef about 5 minutes or until browned.

3 Meanwhile, thinly slice onion and capsicum; add to pan with garlic. Cook, stirring, until onion just softens.

4 Heat tortillas according to directions on packet.

5 Thinly slice avocado. Halve tomatoes.

6 Serve tortillas topped with sour cream, avocado, tomato and beef mixture; accompany with cheese and lime wedges. Sprinkle with fresh coriander leaves, if you like.

prep + cook time 15 minutes
serves 4
nutritional count per serving
45.3g total fat
(15.3g saturated fat); 2662kJ
(636 cal); 23.8g carbohydrate;
31.8g protein; 3.9g fibre

sausages with fresh tomato relish

8 thin beef sausages (640g)

2 tablespoons olive oil

1 small brown onion (80g)

3 teaspoons bottled crushed garlic

1 tablespoon dried italian herbs

1 tablespoon balsamic vinegar

400g (12½ ounces) fresh tomato medley mix

¼ cup (60ml) dry red wine

¼ cup (70g) tomato paste

1 tablespoon light brown sugar

2 x 475g (15-ounce) tubs mashed potato

1 Cook sausages in heated oiled large frying pan, over medium heat, until cooked through.
2 Meanwhile, heat oil in medium frying pan over high heat. Finely chop onion. Cook onion, garlic and dried herbs, stirring, until onion softens. Add vinegar, tomatoes, wine, paste and sugar; bring to the boil. Reduce heat; simmer sauce, uncovered, about 5 minutes or until reduced by half and has thickened. Remove from heat; season to taste.
3 Microwave mashed potato according to directions on tub.
4 Serve sausages with potato; accompany with thick tomato relish. Sprinkle with micro basil before serving, if you like.

prep + cook time 15 minutes **serves** 4
nutritional count per serving 61.6g total fat (28.2g saturated fat); 3507kJ (838 cal); 41.8g carbohydrate; 24.3g protein; 7.1g fibre

gourmet hot dogs with cider-braised onions

4 thick beef sausages (600g)

1 large brown onion (200g)

4 sprigs fresh thyme

¼ cup (60ml) apple cider

1 tablespoon light brown sugar

80g (2½ ounces) smoked cheddar cheese

300g (9½ ounce) packet dry coleslaw

2 tablespoons bottled coleslaw dressing

4 white bread rolls (240g)

2 tablespoons wholegrain mustard

⅓ cup (95g) barbecue sauce

1 Heat oiled barbecue grill plate (or grill pan or barbecue). Cook sausages about 3 minutes each side or until cooked; cut in half lengthways.
2 Meanwhile, thinly slice onion. Cook onion and thyme on heated oiled barbecue flat plate, stirring, about 3 minutes or until onion softens. Add apple cider and sugar; cook, stirring occasionally, about 3 minutes or until onion is caramelised.
3 Thinly slice cheese. Place coleslaw in large bowl; toss through dressing.
4 Split bread rolls lengthways through the top without cutting all the way through; microwave on HIGH (100%) about 30 seconds or until warm. Spread rolls with mustard, fill with sausages, coleslaw, onion and cheese. Accompany with sauce.

prep + cook time 15 minutes **serves** 4
nutritional count per serving 50.6g total fat (23.3g saturated fat); 3446kJ (823 cal); 57.6g carbohydrate; 30.7g protein; 9.3g fibre

note You can use four small baguettes instead of the white rolls, if you prefer.

beef steaks with rocket and sultana salad

1 medium red onion (170g)

¼ cup (60ml) red wine vinegar

1 tablespoon light brown sugar

800g (1½-ounce) piece beef rump steak

1 medium lemon (140g)

1 tablespoon coarsely chopped fresh tarragon

½ cup loosely packed fresh flat-leaf parsley leaves

1 teaspoon dijon mustard

6 drained anchovy fillets

1 teaspoon rinsed, drained capers

40g (1½ ounces) butter

120g (4 ounces) baby rocket leaves (arugula)

⅔ cup (110g) sultanas

2 tablespoons olive oil

1 Thinly slice onion. Combine in medium saucepan with vinegar and sugar; bring to the boil, stirring. Boil, uncovered, stirring occasionally, about 5 minutes or until onion is tender. Remove pickled onion from heat, stand 5 minutes; drain.

2 Heat oiled grill plate (or grill pan or barbecue).

3 Meanwhile, season beef; cook about 5 minutes each side or until cooked as desired. Remove from heat, cover; stand 5 minutes.

4 Finely grate lemon rind (you need 2 teaspoons rind); squeeze juice (you need 1 tablespoon juice). Pound rind, herbs, mustard, anchovies and capers in mortar and pestle until combined. Add butter; pound to combine.

5 Combine rocket, sultanas, pickled onion, juice and oil in large bowl; season to taste.

6 Serve beef topped with butter mixture, accompany with salad.

prep + cook time 15 minutes
serves 4
nutritional count per serving
27.2g total fat (10.8g saturated fat); 2282kJ (546 cal); 27.1g carbohydrate; 47.4g protein; 2.7g fibre

pepperoni veal parmigiana

⅓ cup (80ml) olive oil

4 crumbed veal schnitzels
(400g)

½ cup (130g) bottled tomato
pasta sauce

8 thin pepperoni slices (75g)

1 cup (80g) finely grated
parmesan cheese

200g (6½ ounces) baby green
beans

½ cup loosely packed fresh
flat-leaf parsley leaves

1 lemon (140g)

1 Preheat grill (broiler).
2 Heat half the oil in large frying pan over medium-high heat; cook schnitzels, two at a time, about 1 minute each side or until browned. Drain on absorbent paper. Repeat with remaining oil and schnitzels.
3 Place schnitzels on large oven tray; top with pasta sauce, pepperoni and cheese. Grill about 2 minutes or until cheese is browned lightly and tomato skins begin to burst.
4 Meanwhile, microwave beans until just tender; drain, cover to keep warm.
5 Sprinkle veal with parsley; serve with beans, accompany with lemon cheeks.

prep + cook time 15 minutes
serves 4
nutritional count per serving
57g total fat
(17.2g saturated fat); 2841kJ
(679 cal); 13.3g carbohydrate;
28g protein; 3.6g fibre

veal napolitana

¼ cup (60ml) olive oil

40g (1½ ounces) butter

4 uncrumbed veal schnitzels (400g)

¼ cup (35g) plain (all-purpose) flour

½ cup (80g) seeded black olives

2 cloves garlic, crushed

400g (12½ ounces) canned cherry tomatoes

1 dried bay leaf

1 tablespoon finely chopped fresh oregano

2 medium desiree potatoes (400g)

200g (6½ ounces) cavolo nero

1 fresh long red chilli

¼ cup loosely packed fresh flat-leaf parsley

1 Heat 1 tablespoon of the oil and half the butter in large frying pan over medium heat. Season veal; coat in flour, then shake off excess. Cook veal, in batches, about 30 seconds each side or until cooked as desired; remove from pan, cover to keep warm.

2 Heat 1 tablespoon of the remaining oil in small saucepan over medium heat; cook olives and garlic, stirring, about 1 minute or until fragrant. Add undrained tomatoes and bay leaf; simmer, uncovered, about 5 minutes or until thickened slightly. Stir in oregano; season to taste.

3 Meanwhile, coarsely chop unpeeled potatoes; place in microwave-safe bowl. Microwave potato, covered, on HIGH (100%) for 4 minutes.

4 Coarsely chop cavolo nero. Finely dice chilli. Heat remaining oil and butter in same frying pan. Add potato to pan; cook, stirring, 2 minutes or until potato is golden. Add cavolo nero and chilli to pan; cook until cavolo nero is wilted.

5 Serve veal with vegetables; accompany with tomato and olive mixture.

prep + cook time 15 minutes
serves 4
nutritional count per serving
28.9g total fat (8.6g saturated fat); 2114kJ (505 cal); 28.6g carbohydrate; 29.9g protein; 5.7g fibre

note Cavolo nero is also known as tuscan cabbage, tuscan kale or tuscan black cabbage. It has long, narrow, wrinkled leaves and a rich and astringent, mild cabbage flavour. It doesn't lose its volume like silver beet or spinach when cooked. We used one bunch.

pork

chinese barbecued pork salad

100g (3 ounces) rice vermicelli noodles

4cm (1½-inch) piece fresh ginger (20g)

2 green onions (scallions)

4 king brown mushrooms (320g)

¼ cup (35g) toasted peanuts

1 medium orange (240g)

500g (1 pound) chinese barbecued pork

1 tablespoon hoisin sauce

1 teaspoon light soy sauce

1 tablespoon peanut oil

227g (7 ounces) canned sliced water chestnuts, rinsed, drained

2 teaspoons bottled crushed garlic

8 large iceberg lettuce leaves

2 limes

1 Place noodles in medium heatproof bowl, cover with boiling water; stand until tender, drain.
2 Meanwhile, peel and finely grate ginger. Trim and thinly slice onions. Thinly slice mushrooms. Coarsely chop nuts. Finely grate rind from orange (you need 1 tablespoon rind); squeeze juice (you need ¼ cup juice). Thinly slice pork.
3 To make dressing: Combine rind, juice, sauces and 1 teaspoon of the ginger in screw-top jar; shake well. Season.
4 Heat oil in wok; stir-fry pork, water chestnuts, mushrooms, remaining ginger and garlic over high heat until mushrooms are tender and pork is hot. Add noodles and dressing to pan; toss to combine.
5 Serve pork mixture in lettuce leaves; top with nuts and onion, accompany with lime cheeks.

prep + cook time 15 minutes
serves 4
nutritional count per serving
26.6g total fat
(8.4g saturated fat); 2082kJ
(498 cal); 29.1g carbohydrate;
31g protein; 10.6g fibre

notes Before starting the recipe, boil the kettle so you have boiling water ready to prepare the noodles.
Chinese barbecued pork, also called char siew, is traditionally cooked in special ovens; it has a sweet-sticky coating made from soy sauce, sherry, five-spice powder and hoisin sauce. It's available from chinese butcher shops; ask them to slice it for you.

pork with pineapple and cucumber salsa

2 pork fillets (500g)

2 tablespoons olive oil

2 teaspoons smoked paprika

225g (7 ounces) canned
pineapple pieces

1 lebanese cucumber (130g)

1 fresh long red chilli

¼ cup coarsely chopped
fresh mint

1 tablespoon lime juice

100g salad leaf mix

1 Heat large frying pan over medium heat. Combine pork, oil and paprika in large bowl; season. Cook pork, turning, about 10 minutes or until cooked as desired. Cover; stand 5 minutes.
2 Meanwhile, drain pineapple and chop finely. Finely chop cucumber and chilli. Finely shred mint. Combine pineapple, cucumber, chilli, mint and juice in small bowl; season to taste.
3 Thinly slice pork; serve with salsa and salad leaves.

prep + cook time 15 minutes
serves 4
nutritional count per serving
12.1g total fat
(2.3g saturated fat); 1027kJ
(245 cal); 4.9g carbohydrate;
28.2g protein; 1.7g fibre

five-spice pork cutlets with plum sauce

4 pork cutlets (940g)

1 tablespoon five-spice powder

2 tablespoons peanut oil

1 bunch choy sum (400g)

450g (14½ ounce) packet microwave rice

plum sauce

⅓ cup (75g) firmly packed light brown sugar

½ cup (125ml) water

6 drained canned whole plums (250g)

1 tablespoon chinese cooking wine

1 cinnamon stick

2 star anise

2 tablespoons fish sauce

2 teaspoons malt vinegar

1 Heat large frying pan over medium-high heat. Combine pork, five-spice and oil in large bowl; season. Cook pork about 3 minutes each side or until cooked as desired. Remove from heat, cover; stand 5 minutes.
2 Meanwhile, to make plum sauce: combine sugar and the water in medium saucepan; stir over low heat until sugar dissolves. Discard seeds from plums; add plums to pan with wine, cinnamon and star anise. Bring to the boil, reduce heat; simmer, covered, about 6 minutes or until plums are pulpy. Remove and discard cinnamon stick. Stir in sauce and vinegar; season to taste.
3 Microwave choy sum until just wilted.
4 Microwave rice according to directions on packet.
5 Serve pork with choy sum and rice; drizzle with plum sauce.

prep + cook time 15 minutes
serves 4
nutritional count per serving
16.1g total fat
(4.1g saturated fat); 2282kJ
(545 cal); 58.6g carbohydrate;
37.9g protein; 5.1g fibre

note You can use fresh plums when in season.

sticky maple pork sausages

2 tablespoons olive oil

8 thin pork sausages (650g)

500g (1 pound) frozen peas

2 x 475g (15-ounce) tubs mashed potato

⅓ cup (80ml) pure maple syrup

¼ cup (55g) firmly packed light brown sugar

1 teaspoon dijon mustard

¼ cup (60ml) orange juice

1 Heat oil in large frying pan over medium-high heat; cook sausages, turning, about 10 minutes or until cooked through. Remove from pan.
2 Meanwhile, boil, steam or microwave peas until just tender.
3 Microwave mashed potato according to directions on tub.
4 Combine maple syrup, sugar, mustard and juice in small bowl.
5 Return sausages to pan with syrup mixture; cook about 3 minutes or until syrup is thick.
6 Serve sausages with peas and potato; drizzle with syrup

prep + cook time 15 minutes
serves 4
nutritional count per serving
51.6g total fat
(19.7g saturated fat); 3484kJ
(832 cal); 60.2g carbohydrate;
29.2g protein; 11.5g fibre

note You could also serve the sausages on long bread rolls with pre-made coleslaw and caramelised onion.

bratwurst with cabbage and speck

1 tablespoon olive oil

8 bratwurst sausages (800g)

150g (4½ ounces) speck

¼ large green cabbage (875g)

¾ cup (180ml) chicken stock or water

¼ teaspoon caraway seeds

1 tablespoon wholegrain mustard

1 Heat oil in large frying pan over medium-high heat; cook sausages, turning, about 10 minutes or until browned and cooked through.

2 Meanwhile, cut speck into small batons. Slice cabbage into thin wedges. Heat large saucepan; cook speck, stirring, until browned lightly and crisp. Add cabbage; cook, stirring, until tender. Add stock; simmer, covered, about 3 minutes or until cabbage softens. Stir in caraway seeds and mustard; season to taste.

3 Serve sausages with cabbage mixture.

prep + cook time 15 minutes
serves 4
nutritional count per serving
54.7g total fat
(20.8g saturated fat); 2939kJ
(701 cal); 12.6g carbohydrate;
36.5g protein; 10.7g fibre

spaghettini with hot salami and tomatoes

500g (1 pound) spaghettini pasta

200g (6½ ounces) shaved hot salami

1 fresh long red chilli

1 tablespoon olive oil

2 teaspoons bottled crushed garlic

250g (8 ounces) cherry tomatoes

2 tablespoons rinsed, drained baby capers

1 cup (250ml) dry white wine

⅓ cup loosely packed fresh oregano leaves

½ cup (40g) grated pecorino or parmesan cheese

1 Cook pasta in large saucepan of boiling water until tender; drain. Return to pan.
2 Meanwhile, coarsely chop salami. Finely chop chilli.
3 Heat oil in large frying pan over medium heat; cook salami, stirring, about 2 minutes or until browned and crisp. Remove from pan; cover to keep warm.
4 Cook chilli and garlic in same pan, stirring, about 1 minute or until fragrant. Add tomatoes and capers; cook, stirring, until tomatoes skins begin to burst. Add wine; simmer, uncovered, until liquid is reduced by about a third.
5 Combine salami, sauce mixture and oregano in pan with pasta; cook over low heat until heated through, season to taste. Serve topped with cheese.

prep + cook time 15 minutes
serves 6
nutritional count per serving
18.4g total fat
(5.9g saturated fat); 2144kJ
(513 cal); 58.9g carbohydrate;
18.8g protein; 3.8g fibre

note Before starting the recipe, boil the kettle so you have boiling water ready to go into the saucepan to cook the pasta.

persian-spiced pork with couscous

2 teaspoons ground turmeric

1 teaspoon ground allspice

½ teaspoon ground cardamom

1 tablespoon bottled crushed garlic

2 tablespoons olive oil

600g (1¼ pounds) pork fillet

1 cup (200g) couscous

1 cup (250ml) boiling water

20g (¾ ounce) butter

125g (4 ounces) canned chickpeas (garbanzo beans)

100g (3 ounces) baby spinach leaves

1 lebanese cucumber (130g)

¾ cup (200g) tzatziki dip

½ cup loosely packed fresh mint leaves

1 medium lemon (140g)

1 Heat large oiled frying pan over medium heat. Combine spices, garlic and oil in large bowl; season. Add pork; turn to coat. Cook pork about 5 minutes each side or until cooked. Remove from heat, cover; stand 5 minutes.
2 Meanwhile, combine couscous, the water and butter in medium heatproof bowl, cover; stand about 5 minutes or until liquid is absorbed, fluffing with fork occasionally.
3 Rinse and drain chickpeas; stir chickpeas and spinach through couscous.
4 Slice cucumber into thin batons. Slice pork thickly; serve with couscous, cucumber and tzatziki. Sprinkle over mint; accompany with lemon wedges.

prep + cook time 15 minutes
serves 4
nutritional count per serving
22.1g total fat
(8.1g saturated fat); 2438kJ
(582 cal); 48g carbohydrate;
45g protein; 3.8g fibre

malt vinegar glazed pork

½ cup (125ml) malt vinegar

1 cup (220g) firmly packed light brown sugar

2 teaspoons bottled crushed garlic

1 fresh small red thai (serrano) chilli, sliced thinly

1 tablespoon olive oil

8 pork loin medallions (1kg)

270g (8½-ounce) packet fresh udon noodles

250g (8-ounce) packet rainbow salad mix

¼ cup (60ml) asian noodle dressing

1 cup (80g) snow pea tendrils

1 Heat oil in large frying pan over high heat.

2 Make vinegar glaze by combining vinegar, sugar, garlic and chilli in large bowl.

3 Add pork to pan; cook pork about 2 minutes each side. Pour over vinegar glaze, reduce heat; simmer, turning, about 6 minutes or until pork is cooked and glaze has thickened slightly.

4 Meanwhile, place noodles in large heatproof bowl, cover with boiling water, separate with fork; stand until tender, drain.

5 Meanwhile, combine salad mix and dressing in medium bowl.

6 To serve, place noodles in serving bowls, top with pork and salad; drizzle with pan juices, sprinkle with snow pea tendrils.

prep + cook time 15 minutes **serves** 4
nutritional count per serving 9.2g total fat (2.2g saturated fat); 2785kJ (665 cal); 78.4g carbohydrate; 61.1g protein; 3g fibre

note Before starting the recipe, boil the kettle so you have boiling water ready to prepare the noodles.

peppered pork with fig and sage sauce

2 tablespoons olive oil

4 pork cutlets (940g)

2 teaspoons cracked black pepper

1 cup (200g) dried figs

3 fresh figs (180g)

¼ cup loosely packed fresh sage leaves

1 teaspoon bottled crushed garlic

1½ cups (375ml) apple juice

2 x 475g (15-ounce) tubs mashed potato

1 Heat oil in large frying pan over medium-high heat. Rub pork with pepper; cook pork about 3 minutes each side or until cooked as desired. Remove from pan, cover; stand 5 minutes.
2 Halve dried figs. Quarter fresh figs. Add dried figs to pan with sage, garlic and juice; cook, stirring occasionally, about 3 minutes or until sauce thickens. Stir in fresh figs; season to taste.
3 Meanwhile, microwave potato according to directions on tub.
4 Serve pork and potato drizzled with sauce; sprinkle with extra sage leaves, if you like.

prep + cook time 15 minutes **serves** 4
nutritional count per serving 15.8g total fat (3.7g saturated fat); 1883kJ (450 cal); 41g carbohydrate; 33g protein; 8.1g fibre

asian meatball rolls with hoisin mayonnaise

2 teaspoons vegetable oil

4 thick pork sausages (480g)

¾ cup (225g) mayonnaise

1 tablespoon hoisin sauce

1½ teaspoons finely grated ginger

2 green onions (scallions)

1 fresh long green chilli

1 medium carrot (120g)

4 vietnamese bread rolls (240g)

½ cup (40g) bean sprouts

1 tablespoon sweet chilli sauce

1 Heat oil in large frying pan over medium heat.
2 To make meatballs: chop sausages into 2cm (¾-inch) pieces; cook sausage, stirring, until browned and cooked.
3 Combine mayonnaise, hoisin sauce and ginger in small bowl.
4 Trim onion. Thinly slice onion lengthways. Thinly slice chilli crossways. Peel and thinly slice carrot lengthways.
5 Split rolls without cutting all the way through; spread with mayonnaise. Fill with meatballs, carrot, onion, chilli and sprouts; drizzle over sweet chilli sauce. Accompany with any leftover hoisin mayonnaise.

prep + cook time 15 minutes
makes 4
nutritional count per serving
49.2g total fat
(13.5g saturated fat); 3006kJ
(718 cal); 47.2g carbohydrate;
20.1g protein; 5.8g fibre

notes We used bottled grated ginger available from most supermarkets.
Use a mandoline or V-slicer with a julienne attachment to thinly slice the carrots.

seafood

warm baby octopus salad

2 fresh long red chillies

2 baby fennel bulbs (260g)

3 red radishes (100g)

1 lebanese cucumber (130g)

600g (1¼ pounds) cleaned baby octopus

1 teaspoons bottled crushed garlic

1 cup loosely packed fresh flat-leaf parsley leaves

2 tablespoons lemon juice

⅓ cup olive oil

1 Thinly slice chilli lengthways. Trim fennel and radishes. Using mandoline or V-slicer, thinly slice fennel, radishes and cucumber.

2 Heat oiled grill pan (or grill plate or barbecue) over high heat.

3 Meanwhile, quarter octopus. Combine octopus and garlic in medium bowl; season. Cook octopus about 1 minute or until tender.

4 Combine octopus, fennel, radish, chilli, cucumber, parsley and combined lemon and oil in large bowl; season to taste.

prep + cook time 15 minutes
serves 2
nutritional count per serving
42.2g total fat
(7g saturated fat); 3139kJ
(750 cal); 10g carbohydrate;
78.9g protein; 6.9g fibre

smoked trout and brown rice salad

5 brussels sprouts (350g)
(see notes)

1 small red onion (100g)

250g (8-ounce) packet
microwave brown long-grain rice

1 whole hot-smoked trout
(300g)

2 tablespoons lemon juice

2 tablespoons olive oil

½ teaspoon white (granulated)
sugar

½ cup loosely packed fresh
chervil leaves

1 Bring large pan of hot water
to the boil (see notes).
2 Meanwhile, trim sprouts;
remove outer leaves, reserve.
Cut smaller sprouts into halves;
cut larger sprouts into quarters.
3 Cook sprouts in boiling water
1 minute; add leaves. Immediately
drain into strainer, then plunge
quickly into a large bowl of iced
water; drain immediately. Dry
bowl; return sprouts and leaves
to bowl.
4 Thinly slice onion; add to
sprouts in bowl.
5 Microwave rice according to
directions on packet.
6 Meanwhile, discard skin and
bones from fish; flake flesh
coarsely. Combine with rice.
7 Combine juice, oil and sugar
in screw-top jar; shake well. Add
half to rice mixture; toss gently.
8 Serve trout and rice mixture
with sprout mixture; sprinkle
with chervil. Drizzle salad with
remaining dressing.

prep + cook time 15 minutes
serves 2
nutritional count per serving
24.1g total fat
(3.8g saturated fat); 2316kJ
(553 cal); 47.4g carbohydrate;
31.2g protein; 9.6g fibre

notes Before starting the
recipe, boil the kettle so you
have boiling water ready to
go into the saucepan to blanch
the brussels sprout leaves. You
need to plunge the leaves into
iced water, so make sure you
have some on hand.
You could also use a portion of
cold-smoked, boneless trout, if
you prefer.

buttery garlic prawns

2 fresh long red chillies

2 tablespoons olive oil

100g (3 ounces) butter

400g (12½ ounces) uncooked shelled medium prawns (shrimp)

1 tablespoon bottled crushed garlic

2 tablespoons lime juice

¼ cup loosely packed fresh coriander leaves (cilantro)

1 medium lemon (140g)

1 Finely slice chillies.
2 Heat oil and butter in large frying pan over high heat; cook prawns with chilli, garlic and juice, stirring, about 3 minutes or until prawns just change colour. Season.
3 Sprinkle prawns with coriander; accompany with lemon wedges.

prep + cook time 15 minutes
serves 4
nutritional count per serving
30.3g total fat
(15g saturated fat); 1517kJ
(362 cal); 1.1g carbohydrate;
21g protein; 0.7g fibre

note Serve with microwaved jasmine rice, if you like.

prawn spaghettini

375g (12 ounces) spaghettini pasta

2 fresh long red chillies

2 baby fennel bulbs (260g)

1 medium lemon (140g)

2 tablespoons olive oil

500g (1 pound) uncooked shelled medium king prawns (shrimp)

3 teaspoons bottled crushed garlic

100g (3 ounces) baby rocket leaves (arugula)

1 Cook pasta in large saucepan of boiling water until tender; drain, reserving 1 cup cooking liquid.

2 Meanwhile, thinly slice chilli lengthways. Trim and thinly slice fennel. Finely grate rind from lemon (you need 1 tablespoon rind); juice lemon (you need 2 tablespoons juice).

3 Heat oil in large frying pan over high heat; cook prawns, chilli, fennel and garlic, stirring, 2 minutes. Stir in reserved cooking liquid from pasta, rind and juice; remove from heat. Add pasta and rocket; toss to combine, season to taste.

prep + cook time 15 minutes
serves 4
nutritional count per serving
10.8g total fat
(1.6g saturated fat); 2019kJ
(483 cal); 67.3g carbohydrate;
24.9g protein; 6g fibre

note Before starting the recipe, boil the kettle so you have boiling water ready to go into the saucepan to cook the pasta.

coconut prawns with dipping sauce

vegetable oil, for shallow-frying

½ cup (75g) plain (all-purpose) flour

½ cup (75g) cornflour (cornstarch)

1 teaspoon fine sea salt

1 egg

¾ cup (180ml) water

½ cup (40g) shredded coconut

½ cup (35g) panko (japanese) breadcrumbs

2 tablespoons sesame seeds

650g (1¼ pounds) uncooked medium peeled prawns (shrimp) with tails intact

1 fresh small red thai (serrano) chilli

¼ cup (60ml) lime juice

2 tablespoons light brown sugar

¼ cup (60ml) fish sauce

1 tablespoon sesame oil

2 limes

1 Heat enough oil in large frying pan to come 2cm (¾-inch) up side of pan. Heat oil to medium-high, or 175°C/350°F (a cube of bread dropped into the hot oil will turn golden in about 15 seconds when oil is at the correct temperature).

2 Sift flour, cornflour and salt into large bowl; gradually whisk in combined egg and the water until batter is smooth.

3 Combine coconut, breadcrumbs and sesame seeds in shallow bowl.

4 Dip prawns, in batches, into batter, then into coconut mixture to coat; shallow-fry prawns, in batches, until browned lightly. Drain on absorbent paper. Repeat with remaining prawns, batter and coconut mixture.

5 Meanwhile, finely chop chilli. Combine chilli, juice, sugar, sauce and oil in screw-top jar; shake dressing well.

6 Serve prawns with salad, and sauce for dipping; accompany with lime cheeks, if you like.

prep + cook time 15 minutes
serves 4
nutritional count per serving
17.3g total fat
(7.1g saturated fat); 2105kJ
(503 cal); 43g carbohydrate;
41.5g protein; 3.6g fibre

notes Fishmongers and major supermarkets should have fresh shelled prawns with the tails intact. If you can't find them fresh, prawns are also available frozen. Thaw in the fridge during the day, so they are ready to cook when you get home. Serve prawns with a baby asian salad mix or microwaved rice.

dukkah-crusted salmon

2 tablespoons olive oil

4 skinless salmon fillets (880g)

400g (12½ ounces) baby buk choy

2 x 90g (3-ounce) packets dried ramen noodles

almond dukkah

½ cup (80g) blanched almonds

1 tablespoon each coriander and cumin seeds

¼ cup (35g) sesame seeds

¼ teaspoon black peppercorns

1 Make almond dukkah.
2 Heat oil in same large frying pan over medium heat. Press one side of each fish fillet firmly into dukkah to coat; cook fish 3 minutes each side or until cooked as desired.
3 Meanwhile, quarter buk choy; microwave about 2 minutes or until just tender.
4 Cook noodles in large saucepan of boiling water 4 minutes or until just tender, drain.
5 Serve fish with buk choy and noodles.

ALMOND DUKKAH Dry-fry ingredients in large frying pan, stirring, about 1 minute or until browned lightly and fragrant. Process mixture until chopped coarsely (see notes).

prep + cook time 15 minutes
serves 4
nutritional count per serving
49.3g total fat
(10.3g saturated fat); 3299kJ
(788 cal); 25.7g carbohydrate;
56.6g protein; 9.8g fibre

notes Before starting the recipe, boil the kettle so you have boiling water ready to prepare the noodles.
Dukkah is available from the spice section of most major supermarkets. You can use this instead of making your own, to save even more time.

mussels with beer

vegetable oil for deep frying

500g (1 pound) packet frozen french fries

1 medium zucchini (120g)

1½ cups (375ml) beer

2 teaspoons bottled crushed garlic

1kg (2 pounds) pot-ready mussels

1 cup (250ml) pouring cream

1 tablespoon fresh tarragon leaves

¼ cup finely chopped chives

1 Heat enough oil in large saucepan to come halfway up the side of the pan. Heat oil to medium-high, or 180°C/350°F (a cube of bread dropped into the hot oil will turn golden in about 15 seconds when oil is at the correct temperature).
2 Deep-fry french fries, in batches, according to direction on packet.
3 Meanwhile, cut zucchini into matchsticks.
4 Bring beer to the boil in large saucepan. Add zucchini, garlic and mussels to pan with beer; bring to the boil. Cover; cook about 2 minutes or until mussels start to open.

5 Stir cream and herbs into pan; cook until hot and mussels are open, season. Accompany with french fries.

prep + cook time 15 minutes
serves 2
nutritional count per serving
115.7g total fat
(44.1g saturated fat); 6092kJ
(1455 cal); 62.7g carbohydrate;
25.5g protein; 8.7g fibre

note Use a mandoline or V-slicer with a julienne attachment to cut the zucchini into matchsticks.

quick and easy bouillabaisse

2 cloves garlic

1 litre (4 cups) fish stock

2 x 8cm (3¼-inch) pieces orange peel

2 sprigs fresh thyme

pinch saffron threads

4 uncooked medium prawns (shrimp) (130g)

1 medium fennel bulb (300g)

1 small brown onion (80g)

2 tablespoons olive oil

600g (1¼ pounds) marinara mix

1 long french bread stick (300g)

250g (8 ounces) cherry truss tomatoes

20g (¾ ounce) butter

¼ cup fresh dill leaves

⅓ cup (100g) aïoli

¼ teaspoon cayenne pepper

1 Peel garlic. Keep one clove whole, crush other clove. Combine stock, peel, thyme, whole garlic and saffron in medium saucepan; bring to the boil. Reduce heat, add prawns; simmer, covered, about 4 minutes.

2 Meanwhile, trim and thinly slice fennel. Coarsely chop onion. Heat oil in large saucepan over medium-high heat; cook fennel, onion and crushed garlic, stirring, about 2 minutes or until softened. Add marinara mix; cook, stirring gently, until fish is almost cooked.

3 Preheat grill plate. Slice bread; toast bread on grill plate until browned lightly.

4 Cook truss tomatoes on heated oiled grill plate until just softened.

5 Meanwhile, remove prawns from stock mixture; reserve. Strain stock into marinara mixture; bring to the boil. Remove from heat, stir in butter. Season to taste. Divide bouillabaisse into serving bowls; top with prawns and dill. Sprinkle aïoli with cayenne. Serve bouillabaisse with toast, aïoli and grilled tomatoes.

prep + cook time 15 minutes
serves 4
nutritional count per serving
39.2g total fat
(8.5g saturated fat); 3120kJ
(745 cal); 47.3g carbohydrate;
47.4g protein; 7g fibre

note Use the best fish stock you can get for this recipe as the flavour relies on a good stock.

peri peri prawn and coleslaw tortillas

24 uncooked shelled medium prawns (shrimp) (500g), with tails intact

½ cup (125ml) peri peri sauce

2 tablespoons vegetable oil

1 tablespoon lemon juice

1 tablespoon water

1 cup (300g) mayonnaise

400g (12½ ounces) dry coleslaw vegetable mix

8 x 20cm (8-inch) flour tortillas

½ cup loosely packed fresh coriander (cilantro) leaves

1 Heat oil in grill pan over high heat.

2 Combine prawns and sauce in large bowl; season. Thread prawns onto 24 bamboo skewers. Cook prawns about 3 minutes or until changed in colour.

3 Meanwhile, combine juice, the water and mayonnaise in a large bowl. Add coleslaw mix; toss to combine. Season to taste.

4 Microwave tortillas according to directions on packet. Serve prawns with tortillas and coleslaw. Accompany with lime cheeks, if you like.

prep + cook time 15 minutes
serves 4
nutritional count per serving
39.7g total fat
(5.3g saturated fat); 3093kJ
(740 cal); 58.5g carbohydrate;
34.4g protein; 6.7g fibre

notes Wrap the ends of the skewers in foil to stop them burning during cooking.
If you prefer, you can make your own coleslaw: finely slice a quarter of a green cabbage, 1 carrot and 2 green onions into thin strips; toss through some whole-egg mayonnaise.

honey-mustard prawns

2 tablespoons honey

2 tablespoons dijon mustard

2 tablespoons lemon juice

2 tablespoons olive oil

2 tablespoons water

1 tablespoon bottled crushed garlic

500g (1 pound) uncooked shelled large king prawns (shrimp), with tails intact

8 baby new potatoes (320g)

100g (3 ounces) watercress

2 baby fennel bulbs (260g)

1 small red onion (100g)

1 tablespoon aïoli

1 tablespoon water, extra

1 tablespoon fresh dill sprigs

1 Heat oiled grill plate (or grill pan or barbecue).
2 Combine honey, mustard, juice, oil, the water and garlic in small bowl. Season to taste.
3 Brush prawns with honey mixture; cook, turning and brushing with mixture, about 4 minutes or until prawns are just changed in colour.
4 Meanwhile, quarter unpeeled potatoes; boil, steam or microwave potato until tender.
5 Trim watercress and fennel. Using mandoline and V-slicer, thinly slice fennel and onion.

6 Combine watercress, fennel, onion and potato in medium bowl.
7 Combine aïoli and water. Serve prawns with vegetables; drizzle with aïoli, sprinkle over dill.

prep + cook time 15 minutes
serves 4
nutritional count per serving
14g total fat
(2.1g saturated fat); 1504kJ
(359 cal); 26.5g carbohydrate;
29.6g protein; 4.3g fibre

peppered fish tacos

600g (1¼ pounds) flathead fillets

2 teaspoons cayenne pepper

2 tablespoons vegetable oil

½ cup (120g) sour cream

1 teaspoon finely grated lime rind

1 tablespoon lime juice

2 red radishes (70g)

12 x 15cm (6-inch) corn tortillas

1 cup loosely packed fresh coriander leaves (cilantro)

2 tablespoons drained pickled jalapeños

1 Heat oiled large frying pan over medium heat. Combine fish with rind, cayenne pepper and oil in large bowl; season. Cook fish, turning, about 5 minutes or until cooked.

2 Meanwhile, combine sour cream and juice in small bowl, season to taste. Trim radishes; halve, then slice thinly.

3 Microwave tortillas according to directions on packet.

4 Serve tortillas topped with fish, sour cream mixture, radish, coriander and jalapeños; accompany with lemon wedges, if you like.

prep + cook time 15 minutes **serves** 4
nutritional count per serving 24.2g total fat
(10g saturated fat); 1927kJ (461 cal);
23.1g carbohydrate; 35.8g protein; 3.9g fibre

notes Guests can assemble their own tacos at the table. Serve with grilled corn, if you like.

warm salmon and snow pea salad

1 cup (250ml) light soy sauce

2 tablespoons rice wine vinegar

1 teaspoon sesame oil

600g (1¼ pounds) skinless salmon fillets

200g (6½ ounces) baby buk choy (see note)

2 green onions (scallions)

150g (4½ ounces) snow peas

125g (4 ounces) sugar snap peas

175g (5½ ounces) snow pea tendrils

1 telegraph (hothouse) cucumber (400g)

250g (8 ounces) baby grape tomatoes

1 cup loosely packed fresh mint leaves

2 tablespoons olive oil

1 tablespoon sesame seeds

1 Combine sauce, vinegar and sesame oil in medium saucepan. Cut fish into 5cm (2-inch) pieces; add to pan, stand 5 minutes.
2 Trim buk choy; cut into quarters. Trim onion. Trim and halve snow peas. Trim sugar snap peas and snow pea tendrils. Thinly slice cucumber and onion. Combine buk choy, onion, snow peas, sugar snap peas, cucumber, tomato, tendrils and herbs in large bowl.
3 Heat olive oil in large frying pan over medium heat. Remove fish from marinade, pat dry on absorbent paper; reserve marinade in pan. Cook fish in frying pan about 5 minutes, turning occasionally, until browned lightly and cooked.
4 Meanwhile, bring marinade to the boil; boil, uncovered, 2 minutes.
5 Flake fish into salad; mix through ¼ cup boiled marinade, season. Sprinkle with sesame seeds.

prep + cook time 15 minutes **serves** 4
nutritional count per serving 22.4g total fat (4g saturated fat); 1748kJ (418 cal); 8.7g carbohydrate; 40.1g protein; 8.2g fibre

note You need to buy small baby buk choy as they are tender enough to be eaten raw.

butterflied prawns with garlic butter

500g (1 pound) shelled uncooked king prawns (shrimp), with tails intact

1 tablespoon olive oil

80g (2½ ounces) butter

1 tablespoon bottled crushed garlic

2 tablespoons lemon juice

2 baby cos (romaine) lettuce

1 medium avocado (250g)

1 medium lemon (140g)

1 Butterfly prawns by slicing prawns in half lengthways through back, without cutting all the way through the prawn.

2 Heat oil in large frying pan over medium-high heat. Cook prawns about 1 minute each side or until browned lightly. Add butter and garlic; cook, stirring, about 2 minutes or until fragrant. Stir in juice; season to taste.

3 Halve lettuce. Quarter avocado. Using zester, peel rind in thin strips from lemon (or peel lemon then cut peel into thin strips).

4 Serve prawns with lettuce and avocado; drizzle with garlic butter, sprinkle with rind. Accompany with lemon cheeks, if you like.

prep + cook time 15 minutes
serves 4
nutritional count per serving
32g total fat
(13.9g saturated fat); 1738kJ
(415 cal); 2.6g carbohydrate;
28.1g protein; 3.3g fibre

note Some fishmongers and fish markets sell prawns already butterflied; you can use these instead of preparing your own.

spicy black bean squid stir-fry

1 tablespoon vegetable oil

1 fresh long red chilli

1 green onion (scallion)

1 teaspoon bottled crushed ginger

200g (6½ ounces) squid rings

½ cup (140g) black bean sauce

½ cup each firmly packed fresh mint and coriander (cilantro) leaves

½ cup (40g) bean sprouts

1 Heat oil in wok over high heat.

2 Trim and thinly slice chilli and onion. Stir-fry chilli and ginger 30 seconds. Add squid; stir-fry 30 seconds. Add sauce; stir-fry 1 minute.

3 Serve squid sprinkled with onion, herbs and bean sprouts.

prep + cook time 15 minutes
serves 2
nutritional count per serving
10.6g total fat
(1.6g saturated fat); 732kJ
(175 cal); 1.3g carbohydrate;
17.9g protein; 1.7g fibre

serving suggestion Serve with microwaved jasmine rice.

cheese & egg

creamy zucchini pappardelle

1 large brown onion (200g)

2 small zucchini (180g)

375g (12 ounces) fresh lasagne sheets

1 tablespoon olive oil

100g (3 ounces) pancetta

1 teaspoon bottled crushed garlic

1 cup (250ml) pouring cream

3 eggs

½ cup (40g) finely grated parmesan cheese

¼ cup coarsely chopped fresh flat-leaf parsley

1 Put on water to boil for pasta (see note). Heat oil in large saucepan over high heat.

2 Finely chop onion. Using a vegetable peeler, slice zucchini into long thin ribbons. Cut pasta sheets into long, 5cm (2-inch) wide strips.

3 Cook pasta in boiling water until tender; drain.

4 Cook pancetta, turning, until crisp; remove from pan, cool.

5 Add onion to same pan; cook onion, stirring, until softened. Add garlic and cream to pan; simmer, uncovered, until sauce is reduced by half. Remove from heat; stir in lightly beaten eggs.

6 Add pasta to cream mixture with zucchini and cheese; toss gently. Season to taste. Top pasta with pancetta; sprinkle over parsley. Season, serve immediately.

prep + cook time 15 minutes
serves 4
nutritional count per serving
43.4g total fat
(23.3g saturated fat); 3273kJ
(783 cal); 69.5g carbohydrate;
26.7g protein; 4.9g fibre

note Before starting the recipe, boil the kettle so you have boiling water ready to go into the saucepan to cook the pasta.

quick three-cheese frittata

The frying pan goes under the grill in this recipe, so you need a frying pan with an ovenproof handle, or cover the handle with a few layers of foil to protect it from the heat of the grill.

375g (12 ounces) silver beet (swiss chard)

40g (1½ ounces) butter

8 eggs

⅔ cup (50g) finely grated pecorino cheese

50g (1½ ounces) gorgonzola cheese, crumbled

50g (1½ ounces) firm ricotta cheese

100g (3 ounces) rocket (arugula)

1 tablespoon olive oil

1 tablespoon lemon juice

¼ cup (20g) grated pecorino cheese, extra

1 Preheat grill (broiler).
2 Trim silver beet; shred coarsely. Heat half the butter in 20cm/8-inch (base measurement) frying pan over high heat; cook silver beet, stirring, until wilted. Remove from pan; drain well.
3 Combine eggs, silver beet and pecorino in large jug; season.
4 Melt remaining butter in same pan; pour in egg mixture, top with gorgonzola and ricotta. Cook over medium-low heat until frittata is almost set. Place frittata under grill; grill about 5 minutes or until set and browned lightly.
5 Combine rocket, oil, juice and extra pecorino in medium bowl; serve with frittata. Accompany with warm toast, if you like.

prep + cook time 15 minutes
serves 4
nutritional count per serving
33.9g total fat
(15.8g saturated fat); 1722kJ
(412 cal); 2.3g carbohydrate;
24.3g protein; 2.2g fibre

orange, fennel and haloumi salad

¼ cup (60ml) olive oil

4 baby fennel bulbs (520g)

1 small red onion (100g)

½ cup (125ml) orange juice

1 teaspoon fresh thyme leaves

500g (1 pound) haloumi cheese

100g (3 ounces) rocket (arugula) leaves

3 medium tomatoes (450g)

½ cup loosely packed fresh mint leaves

1 Heat 1 tablespoon of the oil in large frying pan over medium-low heat.
2 Trim fennel; cut into quarters. Thinly slice onion.
3 Cook fennel, cut-side down, in pan about 5 minutes or until browned lightly.
4 Meanwhile, whisk 1 tablespoon of the oil, juice and thyme in small jug until combined; pour over fennel. Add onion to pan, cover with lid or foil; cook, over low heat, until fennel is tender.
5 Slice cheese thickly. Heat remaining oil in large frying pan; cook cheese until browned both sides. Remove from heat.
6 Meanwhile, trim rocket. Thickly slice tomatoes. Arrange rocket on serving platter; top with tomato, fennel mixture and cheese; drizzle with pan juices, sprinkle with mint.

prep + cook time 15 minutes
serves 4
nutritional count per serving
35.5g total fat
(15.7g saturated fat); 2047kJ
(489 cal); 11.3g carbohydrate;
29.8g protein; 4.6g fibre

note Haloumi is a firm, cream-coloured sheep-milk cheese matured in brine; it tastes somewhat like a minty, salty fetta in flavour, and can be grilled or fried, briefly, without breaking down. It should be eaten while still warm as it becomes tough and rubbery on cooling.

welsh rarebit soufflé toasts

8 slices multigrain sourdough bread (560g)

140g (4½ ounces) vintage cheddar cheese

2 green onions (scallions)

1 tablespoon worcestershire sauce

2 teaspoons wholegrain mustard

½ teaspoon cayenne pepper

3 eggs

250g (8 ounces) red grape tomatoes

100g (3 ounces) baby rocket (arugula) leaves

1 Preheat oven to 220°C/425°F.
2 Lightly toast bread. Coarsely grate cheese. Trim and finely chop onions.
3 Combine cheese, onion, sauce, mustard and cayenne pepper in medium bowl.
4 Separate eggs. Add egg yolks to cheese mixture.
5 Beat egg whites in small bowl until soft peaks form. Fold egg whites into cheese mixture; season.
6 Place toast on oven tray; top with cheese mixture. Bake in oven 5 minutes or until cheese is melted and browned lightly.
7 Meanwhile, halve tomatoes; accompany soufflés with tomato and rocket.

prep + cook time 15 minutes
serves 4
nutritional count per serving
19.7g total fat
(9.3g saturated fat); 2332kJ
(558 cal); 65g carbohydrate;
26.8g protein; 7g fibre

classic omelette with smoked cod

200g (6½ ounces) smoked cod

400g (12½ ounces) spinach

8 eggs

1 tablespoon olive oil

40g (1½ ounces) persian fetta cheese, drained

125g (4 ounces) mixed cherry and grape tomatoes

50g (1½ ounces) rocket leaves (arugula)

1 Bring large saucepan of water to the boil; reduce to a simmer (see note).

2 Discard skin from fish. Place fish in baking-paper-lined bamboo steamer or steamer basket over pan of simmering water about 5 minutes or until fish is cooked. Transfer fish to plate; flake flesh with a fork, cover to keep warm.

3 Meanwhile, trim spinach. Boil, steam or microwave spinach until wilted; drain. When cool enough to handle, squeeze out excess liquid.

4 Whisk 4 eggs in small jug; season. Melt half the oil in heated medium frying pan; pour in egg mixture, tilting to coat base of pan. Cook over high heat until egg is almost set; top one half of the omelette with half the fish and half the spinach, crumble over half the cheese. Carefully tilt pan and fold omelette over filling; slide omelette onto serving plate, cover to keep warm. Repeat to make a second omelette.

5 Quarter tomatoes. Combine rocket and tomato in small bowl. Serve omelettes with salad.

prep + cook time 15 minutes
serves 2
nutritional count per serving
57.4g total fat
(29.5g saturated fat); 3172kJ
(758 cal); 3.6g carbohydrate;
55.1g protein; 6.6g fibre

notes Before starting the recipe, boil the kettle so you have boiling water ready to go into the saucepan to steam the fish.

cheesy prosciutto rice cakes

450g (14½-ounce) packet microwave white long-grain rice

2 slices prosciutto (30g)

½ cup (60g) frozen peas

2 teaspoons finely grated lemon rind

¼ cup finely chopped fresh chives

1½ cups (150g) coarsely grated mozzarella cheese

2 eggs

½ cup (50g) packaged breadcrumbs

⅓ cup (80ml) olive oil

100g (3 ounces) mixed salad leaves

1 cup (320g) tomato or capsicum relish

1 Bring kettle of water to the boil.

2 Meanwhile, microwave rice according to packet directions.

3 Coarsely chop prosciutto.

4 Place peas in small heatproof bowl, cover with boiling water. Stand 1 minute, then drain. Combine peas, rice, prosciutto, rind, chives, cheese, eggs and breadcrumbs in large bowl; season.

5 Heat half the oil in large frying pan over medium heat. Using wet hands, shape ¼-cups of rice mixture into patties. Cook patties, in batches, about 2 minutes each side or until browned and cooked through. Repeat to make a total of 12 patties. Serve patties with salad leaves; accompany with tomato relish.

prep + cook time 15 minutes
serves 4
nutritional count per serving
30.1g total fat
(9g saturated fat); 2447kJ
(585 cal); 54.6g carbohydrate;
21g protein; 3.9g fibre

chorizo and tomato omelette with chilli beans

The frying pan goes under the grill in this recipe, so you need a frying pan with an ovenproof handle, or cover the handle with a few layers of foil to protect it from the heat of the grill.

420g (13½ ounces) canned chilli beans

1 cured chorizo sausage (170g)

125g (4 ounces) cherry tomatoes

1 tablespoon olive oil

6 eggs

2 tablespoons milk

¼ cup (30g) coarsely grated cheddar cheese

¼ cup loosely packed fresh flat-leaf parsley leaves

1 Preheat grill (broiler).
2 Place undrained beans in medium microwave-save bowl; cover. Microwave on HIGH (100%) for 2 minutes, stirring halfway through cooking time.
3 Meanwhile, heat oil in large ovenproof frying pan over medium-high heat.
4 Thinly slice chorizo. Halve tomatoes. Cook chorizo and tomato, stirring, until chorizo is browned and crisp.
5 Meanwhile, whisk eggs, milk and cheese in large bowl until combined; season. Pour egg mixture into pan, tilting to cover base of pan. Cook, over low heat, about 5 minutes. Place pan under grill for 1 minute or until just set.
6 Cut omelette into wedges; sprinkle with parsley. Serve with chilli beans.

prep + cook time 15 minutes
serves 4
nutritional count per serving
27.8g total fat (9.4g saturated fat); 1793kJ (429 cal); 17.1g carbohydrate; 24.4g protein; 7.7g fibre

buttermilk mac 'n' cheese

250g (8 ounces) macaroni pasta

1¼ cups (300g) sour cream

1½ cups (375ml) buttermilk

½ teaspoon ground nutmeg

2½ cups (250g) pizza cheese

½ cup (35g) panko (japanese) breadcrumbs

1 tablespoon fresh thyme leaves

1 Cook pasta in large saucepan of boiling water until tender; drain.
2 Heat sour cream and buttermilk in large saucepan over low heat; stir in nutmeg and about three-quarters of the cheese, stir until smooth. Season.
3 Preheat grill (broiler).
4 Meanwhile, combine remaining cheese, breadcrumbs and thyme in small bowl. Stir pasta into hot cheese sauce; spoon into oiled 2-litre (8-cup) ovenproof dish. Sprinkle with breadcrumb mixture.
5 Grill about 2 minutes or until browned lightly.

prep + cook time 15 minutes
serves 4
nutritional count per serving
46.4g total fat
(29.8g saturated fat); 3243kJ
(775 cal); 55.9g carbohydrate;
32g protein; 2.5g fibre

notes Before starting the recipe, boil the kettle so you have boiling water ready to go into the saucepan to cook the pasta. Accompany with a green leafy salad, if you like.

three-cheese carbonara

750g (1½ pounds) fresh spinach and ricotta agnolotti

2 egg yolks

¾ cup (180ml) pouring cream

180g (5½ ounces) cherry bocconcini cheese, torn in half

60g (2 ounces) gorgonzola cheese, crumbled

½ cup (40g) finely grated parmesan cheese

2 green onions (scallions)

1 tablespoon toasted pine nuts

100g (3 ounces) beetroot leaves or mixed salad greens

1 Cook pasta in large saucepan of boiling water until tender; drain, reserving ½ cup cooking liquid.
2 Whisk egg yolks, cream, bocconcini, gorgonzola, half the parmesan and the reserved cooking liquid in a medium bowl until combined. Trim and thinly slice onions; reserve green part.
3 Return pasta to pan, add egg mixture and onion; cook, stirring, over low heat, about 2 minutes or until cheese melts. Season to taste.
4 Serve pasta sprinkled with remaining parmesan, reserved green onion and nuts; accompany with beetroot leaves.

prep + cook time 15 minutes
serves 6
nutritional count per serving
31.8g total fat
(18.8g saturated fat); 1894kJ
(452 cal); 20.4g carbohydrate;
20.6g protein; 2.4g fibre

notes Before starting the recipe, boil the kettle so you have boiling water ready to go into the saucepan to cook the pasta.

cooking techniques

Trimming watercress This peppery green is grown in water; use scissors to cut off the roots then pull the leaves off any thick woody stems.

To prepare asparagus, snap the woody end off the asparagus by holding the stem close to the base and bending it until it snaps. Discard the woody end. Trim the outer skin with a vegetable peeler.

When cutting a chilli on the diagonal, leave it whole. The seeds are the heat source, so if you are intolerant of high heat levels, remove the seeds and membranes, or use less chilli.

To chop a shallot, cut it in half through the root, making horizontal and vertical cuts in each half, but don't cut all the way through; chop finely.

To remove corn from fresh cobs, remove the husk (the outer covering) and the silk (the soft silky inner threads), and trim one side of the corn cob so it lies flat. Use a large flat-bladed knife to cut down the cob, close to the core, to remove the kernels.

To trim green onions, pull the papery skin, towards the root, off the onion. Cut the root end off, then slice the white end of the onion as directed by the recipe. The green end can be used to garnish the dish, either thinly sliced, or curled by placing thin strips into iced water.

To crush garlic, press unpeeled garlic firmly with the flat blade of a large knife (top) crushing the clove. Pull off the papery skin and chop the clove finely with the knife. A garlic press (bottom) removes and leaves the skin behind while crushing the garlic.

To toast sesame seeds in a wok or small frying pan, place seeds over medium heat; stir seeds, constantly, until fragrant and golden, about 3-5 minutes. Remove immediately from pan.

To shed a cabbage, cut it in half, then peel and discard the outer leaves. Use a large flat-bladed knife to cut the cabbage into thin slices.

Cutting cucumbers into ribbons will give thin, uniform slices. The best tool for this is a vegetable peeler. Applying more pressure on the peeler gives thicker ribbons.

To slice a capsicum, cut the top and bottom off and stand it on one end; slice down removing all the flesh. Remove and discard the seeds and membranes, and slice the flesh as indicated by the recipe.

Chiffonade is a way of cutting green leaves into long, thin strips. Lay leaves flat on top of each other, then roll up tightly and cut into thin slices.

To trim snow peas, use a sharp knife to trim the ends from the snow pea, then pull to remove the thin string from one side of the pea. Use whole, or slice the snow peas thinly as directed by the recipe.

To extract the seeds and pulp from a pomegranate, cut it in half and hold it over a bowl. Hit it sharply with a spoon – the seeds (which are surrounded by the pulp) should fall out – if they don't, dig them out with a teaspoon. Be careful, as the pomegranate juice can stain your hands, cloths and bench top.

Deveining a prawn (1) is done to remove its digestive membrane (the 'vein' in question). While it may be left in, it can result in a gritty taste. First, shell the prawn, then use a small sharp knife to make a slit along the middle of the back, from the head to the tail, to expose the dark vein.

To devein a prawn (2), lift and remove the exposed vein with your fingers. If you're having problems grasping the vein with your fingers, it may be easier to use a wooden skewer – slip it underneath the vein then lift the vein up and out.

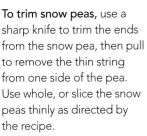

glossary

AIOLI a garlic mayonnaise; available from supermarkets and delis.

ALLSPICE also known as pimento or jamaican pepper; available whole or ground. Tastes like a blend of clove, cinnamon and nutmeg – all spices.

ASIAN SALAD MIX also sold as mixed baby asian greens; a packaged mix of baby buk choy, choy sum, gai lan and water spinach. Available from Asian food stores and most supermarkets.

BABA GHANOUSH a roasted eggplant (aubergine) dip or spread.

BACON, SHORTCUT a 'half rasher'; the streaky (belly), narrow portion of the rasher has been removed leaving the choice cut eye meat (fat end).

BALSAMIC GLAZE see vinegar.

BEANS, WHITE in this book, some recipes may simply call for 'white beans', a generic term we use for canned or dried cannellini, haricot, navy or great northern beans, all of which can be substituted for the other.

BEEF
chipolata also known as 'little fingers'; highly spiced, coarse-textured sausage.
fillet steaks a tender cut from the lower portion of the ribs (sirloin).
minute steak boneless beef, very thin, and usually scored and pounded to tenderise it. Because of its small size, it usually requires only a minute per side to cook, using high heat.
rump steak medallions rump is a boneless cut taken from the upper part of the hindquarter. Medallions are a crossways cut.
scotch fillet steaks also known as beef rib-eye steaks. Cut from the muscle running behind the shoulder along the spine.
sirloin steak cut from the lower part of the ribs just in front of the rump.

BRATWURST usually refers to a sausage made from pork in a natural casing that is either grilled or fried in a pan. Very popular in Germany, with each region having its own specialty. Available both cooked (pale and stiff) and raw (pink in colour).

BREAD
tortillas thin, round unleavened bread. Two kinds are available, one made from wheat and the other from corn (maize).
turkish also known as pide; comes in long (about 45cm) flat loaves as well as individual rounds.
vietnamese rolls a torpedo or baguette-shaped roll.

BREADCRUMBS
packaged fine-textured, crunchy, purchased white breadcrumbs.
panko also known as japanese breadcrumbs. Have a lighter texture than Western-style breadcrumbs. Available from Asian grocery stores and many major supermarkets. Unless you make rather coarse breadcrumbs from white bread that's either quite stale or gently toasted, nothing is an adequate substitution. Gives a crunchy texture with a delicate, pale golden colour.
stale one- or two-day-old bread made into crumbs by grating, blending or processing.

BUTTER use salted or unsalted (sweet) butter; 125g is equal to one stick (4 ounces) of butter.
unsalted often called 'sweet' butter, simply has no added salt. It is mainly used in baking, and if the recipe calls for unsalted butter, then it should not be substituted.

BUTTERMILK originally the term given to the slightly sour liquid left after butter was churned from cream, today it is commercially made similarly to yogurt. Sold alongside all fresh milk products in supermarkets; despite the implication of its name, it is low in fat.

CAJUN SEASONING used to give an authentic American deep-south spicy cajun flavour to food. This packaged blend of assorted herbs and spices can include paprika, basil, onion, fennel, thyme, cayenne and tarragon.

CAPERS the grey-green buds of a warm climate (usually Mediterranean) shrub, sold either dried and salted or pickled in a vinegar brine. Baby capers, those picked early, are very small, fuller-flavoured and more expensive than the full-size one. Capers, whether packed in brine or in salt, must be rinsed well before using.

CARAWAY SEEDS available in seed or ground form. Has a pungent aroma and a sweet, but tangy, flavour.

CARDAMOM purchase in pod, seed or ground form. Has a distinctive aromatic, sweetly rich flavour.

CAYENNE PEPPER a long, thin-fleshed, extremely hot red chilli usually sold dried and ground.

CELERIAC (celery root) tuberous root with a brown skin, white flesh and a celery-like flavour. It has a soft, velvety flesh that has the creaminess of potato when mashed, with a subtle celery flavour.

CHEESE
cheddar, smoked a hard cheddar cheese which has been placed, uncut, in a smoke room for about six hours. There is also artificially smoked cheese where flavour is added to the milk before the cheese is made. Available from major supermarkets and specialist cheese stores.
cheddar, vintage has a smooth, fairly hard texture; its long maturing process gives a strong lingering flavour.
fetta Greek in origin; a crumbly textured goat or sheep-milk cheese with a sharp, salty taste.
fetta, persian is a soft, creamy fetta marinated in a blend of olive oil, garlic, herbs and spices.
haloumi a firm, cream-coloured sheep-milk cheese matured in brine; somewhat like a minty, salty fetta in flavour, haloumi can be grilled or fried, briefly, without breaking down. Should be eaten while still warm as it becomes tough and rubbery on cooling.
pecorino is the generic Italian name for cheeses made from sheep milk. It's a hard, white to pale yellow cheese.
pizza a blend of grated mozzarella, cheddar and parmesan.

CHICKEN BREAST, SMOKED ready-to-eat smoked chicken, available as a whole small bird or breasts. Sold cryovac-packed in supermarkets.

CHICKPEAS also called garbanzos, channa or hummus; round, sandy-coloured legume.

CHILLI available in many different types and sizes. Use rubber gloves when seeding and chopping fresh chillies as they can burn your skin. Removing seeds and membranes lessens the heat level.

green any unripened chilli; also some particular varieties that are ripe when green, such as jalapeño or habanero.
jalapeño fairly hot green chillies, available bottled in brine or fresh from specialty greengrocers. We used the medium-hot, sweetish chopped bottled version in our recipes.
korean red pepper paste a Korean peanut chilli sauce; available from Asian grocery stores. May also be labelled as 'gochujang'.
long (green and red) available both fresh and dried; a generic term used for any moderately hot, long (about 6cm to 8cm), thin chilli.
powder (ground) the Asian variety is the hottest, made from ground chillies; it can be used as a substitute for fresh chillies in the proportion of ½ teaspoon ground chilli powder to 1 medium chopped fresh chilli.
thai also known as 'scuds'; tiny, very hot and bright red in colour.

CHINESE BARBECUED PORK also called char siew. Traditionally cooked in special ovens, this pork has a sweet-sticky coating made from soy sauce, sherry, five-spice powder and hoisin sauce. Available from Asian food stores.

CHINESE COOKING WINE made from rice, wheat, sugar and salt, with 13.5% alcohol; available from Asian food stores. Mirin or sherry can be substituted.

CHORIZO SAUSAGE of Spanish origin, made of coarsely ground pork and highly seasoned with garlic and chilli. They are deeply smoked, very spicy and dry-cured. Also available raw.

CLOVES dried flower buds of a tropical tree; available whole or ground.

CORIANDER also known as pak chee, cilantro or chinese parsley; bright-green leafy herb with a pungent flavour. Both the stems and roots of coriander are also used in Thai cooking; wash well before using. Also available ground or as seeds; these should not be substituted for fresh coriander as the tastes are completely different.

CORNFLOUR also known as cornstarch; used as a thickening agent. Available as 100% maize (corn) and wheaten cornflour.

COUSCOUS a fine, grain-like cereal product made from semolina; a dough of semolina flour and water is sieved then dehydrated to produce minuscule even-sized pellets of couscous; it is rehydrated by steaming, or with the addition of a warm liquid, and swells to three or four times its original size.
israeli couscous also known as pearl couscous, is made of baked wheat rather than semolina (like the couscous from North Africa). Its granules are much larger (its size and shape is similar to a pearl) and it maintains its texture and firmness without sticking.

CREAM unless otherwise stated we use fresh cream, also known as pouring and pure cream; it has no additives unlike commercially thickened cream. Minimum fat content of 35%.
sour a thick commercially-cultured soured cream, with a minimum fat content of 35%.
thickened (heavy) a whipping cream containing a thickener, with a minimum fat content of 35%.

CRÈME FRAÎCHE mature fermented cream having a slightly tangy, nutty flavour and velvety texture. Used in savoury and sweet dishes. Minimum fat content of 35%.

CUMIN ground spice also known as zeera or comino.

CURRANTS, DRIED tiny, seedless, almost black raisins so-named after a grape variety that originated in Corinth, Greece. Not the same as fresh currants.

DAIKON also known as giant white radish. Used extensively in Japanese cooking; has a sweet, fresh flavour without the bite of the common red radish; can be used raw in salads and as a garnish, or cooked in various ways.

DUKKAH an Egyptian spice blend made of roasted nuts and aromatic spices. It is available from Middle-Eastern food stores, specialty spice stores and some supermarkets.

EGGS some recipes in this book may call for raw or barely cooked eggs; exercise caution if there is a salmonella problem in your area. The risk is greater for those who are pregnant, elderly or very young, and those with impaired immune systems.

FIVE-SPICE POWDER a fragrant mixture of ground cinnamon, cloves, star anise, sichuan pepper and fennel seeds. Also known as chinese five-spice.

FLAT-LEAF PARSLEY a flat-leaf variety of parsley also known as continental or italian parsley.

GARAM MASALA a blend of spices based on varying proportions of cardamom, cinnamon, coriander, cloves, fennel and cumin, roasted and ground together. Black pepper and chilli can be added for a hotter version.

GHEE a type of clarified butter; whereby the milk solids are cooked until they are a golden brown, which imparts a nutty flavour and sweet aroma; this fat can be heated to a high temperature without burning.

GINGER also known as green or root ginger; the thick root of a tropical plant. Can be kept, peeled, covered with dry sherry in a jar and refrigerated, or frozen in an airtight container.
pickled pink available, packaged, from Asian groceries; pickled paper-thin shavings of ginger in a mixture of vinegar, sugar and natural colouring.

HORSERADISH CREAM commercially prepared creamy paste made of grated horseradish, vinegar, oil and sugar.

HUMMUS a Middle-Eastern salad or dip made from softened dried chickpeas, garlic, lemon juice and tahini (sesame seed paste); can be purchased, ready-made, from most delicatessens and supermarkets.

LEEK a member of the onion family, resembles the green onion but is much larger and more subtle and mild in flavour.

MAPLE SYRUP a thin syrup distilled from the sap of the maple tree. Maple-flavoured syrup or pancake syrup is not an adequate substitute for the real thing.

MARINARA MIX mixture of uncooked, chopped seafood available from fish markets and fishmongers.

MIRIN a champagne-coloured Japanese cooking wine made of glutinous rice and alcohol; used expressly for cooking and should not be confused with sake.

MUSHROOMS

king brown a strong, rich and meaty mushroom.

portobello mature swiss browns. Large, dark brown mushrooms with full-bodied flavour, ideal for filling or barbecuing.

MUSTARD

english an extremely hot powdered mustard containing ground mustard seeds (both black or brown and yellow-white), wheat flour and turmeric. This mustard is also available in a milder, less hot, version.

wholegrain also known as seeded mustard. A French-style coarse-grain mustard made from crushed mustard seeds and dijon-style french mustard.

NANAMI TOGARASHI a powdered chilli mix; available from Asian grocery stores, and specialist spice shops.

NORI (toasted seaweed) is a type of dried seaweed used in Japanese cooking to make sushi. Sold in thin sheets, plain or toasted (yaki-nori).

PANCETTA is lean pork belly first salted and cured then spiced and rolled into a fat loaf.

POLENTA also known as cornmeal. A flour-like cereal made of dried corn (maize) sold ground in several different textures; also the name of the dish made from it.

QUAILS a small, delicate flavoured, domestically grown game bird ranging in weight from 250g to 300g; also known as partridge.

QUINCE PASTE a very thick jam made from quince. Deep-red to orange in colour, and has a very rich sweet taste and a slightly floral flavour. Available from gourmet food stores and some larger supermarkets.

SAUCES

barbecue a spicy, tomato-based sauce used to marinate, baste or as an accompaniment.

black bean a Chinese-style sauce made from fermented soya beans, spices, water and wheat flour.

fish called naam pla on the label if it is Thai made; the Vietnamese version, nuoc naam, is almost identical. Made from pulverised salted fermented fish (most often anchovies); has a pungent smell and strong taste. There are many versions of varying intensity, so use according to your taste.

hoisin a thick, sweet and spicy Chinese-style barbecue sauce made from salted fermented soya beans, onions and garlic.

peri peri (piri piri) an African word for chilli and also a hot chilli sauce used in Portuguese and African cookery.

soy made from fermented soya beans. Several variations are available in most supermarkets and Asian food stores. We use a mild Japanese variety in our recipes; possibly the best table soy and the one to choose if you only want one variety.

japanese an all-purpose low-sodium soy sauce made with more wheat content than its Chinese counterparts; fermented in barrels and aged.

light soy a fairly thin, pale but salty tasting sauce; used in dishes in which the natural colour of the ingredients is to be maintained. Don't confuse with salt-reduced or low-sodium soy sauces.

sweet chilli a comparatively mild, Thai-style sauce made from red chillies, sugar, garlic and vinegar.

taco available hot or mild. Made with varying amounts of tomato paste, jalapeno chillies, vinegar, salt, cumin, other spices and onions.

teriyaki a Japanese-style sauce made from soy sauce, mirin, sugar, ginger and other spices.

tomato pasta made from a blend of tomatoes, herbs and spices.

worcestershire a dark coloured condiment made from garlic, soy sauce, tamarind, onions, molasses, lime, anchovies, vinegar and other seasonings.

SAUSAGES minced meat seasoned with salt and spices, mixed with cereal and packed into casings. Also known as snags or bangers.

SILVER BEET also known as swiss chard and mistakenly called spinach; a member of the beet family grown for its tasty green leaves and celery-like stems. Best cooked rather than eaten raw. Also known as blettes.

SNOW PEAS also called mange tout ('eat all'). *Snow pea tendrils*, are the growing shoots of the plant, and are sold by greengrocers, and *snow pea sprouts* are the tender new growths of snow peas; also known as mange tout.

SPECK is made from cured and smoked boned hind pork leg with a smoky flavour.

SPINACH is also known as english spinach. Its thick, soft oval leaves and green stems are both edible. Baby spinach is also available.

STAR ANISE a dried star-shaped fruit of a tree native to China. The pods, which have an astringent aniseed or liquorice flavour, are widely used in the Asian kitchen. Available whole and ground, it is an essential ingredient in five-spice powder.

SULTANAS dried grapes, also known as golden raisins.

TELEGRAPH CUCUMBER (hothouse) also known as the european or burpless cucumber; slender and long (35cm and more), its thin dark-green skin has shallow ridges running down its length.

TZATZIKI is a Greek yogurt dip made with cucumber, garlic and sometimes chopped fresh mint. You can buy tzatziki ready-made in supermarkets and delicatessens.

VEAL SCHNITZEL is thinly sliced steak available crumbed or plain (uncrumbed); we use plain schnitzel, which are sometimes called escalopes, in our recipes.

VINEGAR

balsamic has a deep rich brown colour with a sweet and sour flavour. Originally from Modena, Italy, there are now many balsamic vinegars on the market ranging in pungency and quality depending on how long they have been aged. Quality can be determined up to a point by price; use the most expensive sparingly.

balsamic glaze a thick reduction of balsamic vinegar; also called crema or balsamic reduction, it is made from grape must (the freshly pressed grape juice from young grapes containing the skins, seeds, and stems of the fruit) and balsamic vinegar. The best will have no added sugar or preservatives.

brown malt made from fermented malt and beech shavings.

cider (apple cider) made from fermented apples.

red wine based on a blend of fermented red wines.

rice wine made from rice wine lees (sediment left after fermentation), salt and alcohol.

white wine made from a blend of white wines.

WATER CHESTNUTS resembles a chestnut in appearance, hence the English name. They are small brown tubers with a crisp, white, nutty-tasting flesh. Their crunchy texture is best experienced fresh, however, canned water chestnuts are more easily found and can be kept about a month, once opened, under refrigeration.

WHITE MISO PASTE Japan's famous bean paste made from fermented soya beans and rice, rye or barley. It varies in colour, texture and saltiness. White miso tends to have a sweeter and somewhat less salty flavour than the darker red miso. Dissolve the miso in a little bit of water before adding. Keeps well refrigerated.

ZUCCHINI also known as courgette.

index

Published in 2013 by ACP Books, Sydney

ACP Books are published by ACP Magazines Limited

a division of Nine Entertainment Co.

54 Park St, Sydney

GPO Box 4088, Sydney, NSW 2001.

phone (02) 9282 8618; fax (02) 9126 3702

acpbooks@acpmagazines.com.au; www.acpbooks.com.au

ACP BOOKS

Publishing Director, ACP Magazines - Gerry Reynolds

Publisher - Sally Wright

Editorial and Food Director - Pamela Clark

Creative Director - Hieu Chi Nguyen

Published and Distributed in the United Kingdom by Octopus Publishing Group

Endeavour House

189 Shaftesbury Avenue

London WC2H 8JY

United Kingdom

phone (+44)(0)207 632 5400; fax (+44)(0)207 632 5405

info@octopus-publishing.co.uk;

www.octopusbooks.co.uk

Printed by Toppan Printing Co., China

International foreign language rights, Brian Cearnes, ACP Books bcearnes@acpmagazines.com.au

A catalogue record for this book is available from the British Library.

ISBN: 978-174245-352-1 (pbk.)

© ACP Magazines Ltd 2013

ABN 18 053 273 546

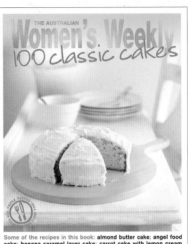

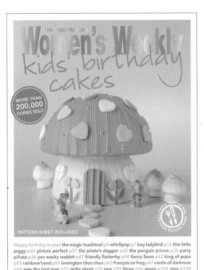